JAZZ WRITINGS

JAZZ WRITINGS

ESSAYS AND REVIEWS 1940–84

Philip Larkin

Edited by Richard Palmer and John White

continuum
LONDON • NEW YORK

Continuum

The Tower Building   15 East 26th Street
11 York Road   Suite 1703
London SE1 7NX   New York
                           NY 10010

Originally published in 1999 in hardcover as *Reference Back: Philip Larkin's Uncollected Jazz Writings 1940–84* by The University of Hull Press as part of its Philip Larkin Society Monographs series.

Published in paperback in 2001 by Continuum by arrangement with Bayou Press Ltd.

This edition 2004, Reprinted 2005

British Library Cataloguing-in-Publication Data
A catalogue record for this book is available from the British Library.

ISBN 08264 76996 (paperback)

Library of Congress Cataloging-in-Publication Data
Larkin, Philip.
[Reference back]
Larkin's jazz: essays & reviews, 1940–84 / edited by Richard Palmer and John White.
p. cm.
Originally published: Reference back : Philip Larkin's uncollected jazz writings, 1940–84. Hull : Hull University Press, 1999. (Philip Larkin Society monographs)
Includes bibliographical references (p.) and index.
1. Jazz—History and criticism. 2. Sound recordings—Reviews.
I. Palmer, Richard, 1947– II. White, John, 1939– III. Title.

ML3507 .L42 2001
781.65'09—dc21
00-047599

Typeset by Interactive Sciences Ltd, Gloucester
Printed and bound in Great Britain by Antony Rowe, Chippenham, Wiltshire

Contents

Acknowledgements

The editors wish to thank the following people and institutions for their help: Barry Bloomfield, the late Michael Bowen, Frances Hackeson, John Osborne, Alan Plater, Anthony Thwaite, (whose initial provision of materials ignited the project), Michael Tucker, Steve Voce, James Booth and The Philip Larkin Society, and the Headmaster and Governors of Bedford School for the grant of a sabbatical term to Richard Palmer in the summer of 1998 which greatly facilitated the writing of this book.

We are grateful for the expert assistance received from The Brynmor Jones Library, University of Hull, especially the staff of the Philip Larkin Room; the Reference Department staff, Bedford Central Library; the Periodicals Department staff, Cambridge University Library; and the Archivist, *Daily Telegraph*.

Philip Larkin's entry on Duke Ellington appeared in *Makers of Modern Culture*, ed. Justin Wintle (Routledge & Kegan Paul Ltd, 1968, pp. 155–6), and is reprinted with kind permission of the publishers.

Every effort has been made to trace or contact the copyright holders of original material contained in this volume.

Foreword
by Alan Plater

Nobody ever got rich and famous writing jazz criticism. It is a labour of love and this collection contains massive proportions of both; but what survives of them is love.

The labour is implied: the books read and absorbed, the music listened to – quite apart from the records on the immediate syllabus – the range of scholarship, Gibbon rubbing shoulders with Hardy. Plus, of course, the labour that went into that acute, finely honed prose. It may have been mere journalism according to Philip's own wry assessment but consider this:

> Fats Waller's face . . . was the kind that you can carve on an orange; squeeze it one way and it laughs, another and it weeps or looks puzzled.

There's nothing mere about that; there's a poet at work.

Thirty or even, in some cases, forty years on, this collection goes a long way towards reclaiming Philip from the demonologists (Chandler used to call them 'primping second-guessers') who fell on the *Selected Letters* and the biography with evangelical zeal and pronounced him unfit for human consumption on the basis of racism, sexism and various other disorders lumped together under any other business on that day's agenda.

Well, here is our designated demon on the racist issue, writing in 1969:

> It is an irony almost too enormous to be noticed that the thorough penetration of Anglo-Saxon civilisation by Afro-American culture by means of popular music is a direct, though long-term, result of the abominable slave trade.

And on the sexist issue, at the end of a review of books about Bessie Smith and Billie Holiday in 1973, he writes:

> Different in their styles, similar in their quality, these two women gave the world more than it could ever have repaid, even if it had tried.

Here are two huge, compassionate truths wrapped up in a sentence apiece, each informed by decency and anger, and enough to start a revolution any day of the week.

Philip is a grown-up critic in the true sense of the word, seeing praise as a crucial area of responsibility. In the modern jargon, he has attitude and we know where he's coming from. He's coming from his late teens and early twenties, a smoky room listening to early Armstrong and Ellington, Pee Wee Russell and Fats Waller, and of course, the blues, 'the most important cultural phenomenon since modernism'.

His early antipathy towards Parker, Mingus, Coltrane and all that followed could hardly be better documented; after all, he wrote his own documents. But in this collection, we see a softening of attitudes. Ornette Coleman's 'Chappaqua Suite' even crops up among his records of the year for 1967. Indeed, these selections, made for the *Daily Telegraph* between 1961 and 1970 and included here for the benefit of anoraked enthusiasts like me, stand up to scrutiny astonishingly well. It would be instructive to compare them with parallel listings of the time in, say, film, television, books or the theatre. Anybody who bought half these records would have a damn good collection. I did and I have, though not because Philip told me to.

As a critic he was big enough to change his mind, but also smart enough to sniff the crap at a hundred paces, especially when it was on the page. He is deeply intolerant of flabby prose and socio/econo/historical babble masquerading as thought. In that sense, he never ceases to be an Oxford man.

He maintains his passion but he always keeps his intellectual cool. He shows proper awe towards Whitney Balliett of the *New Yorker*, a jazz reporter of genius with the soul and pen of a poet, the man who wrote of Dizzy Gillespie, 'He liked to blow the grass flat and divide the waters.' But Balliett, Philip continues, cannot be considered a true critic since he in turn is in total awe of the musicians and cannot bear to say a bad word about any of them.

Moving down several divisions into the minor leagues, Philip reserves his top-quality scorn for the pseuds and second-guessers. He says of a couple of American writers that they are 'so square they could play snooker with dice'. And, as in life, he is at his best with the glancing blows, thrown away *en passant*, of 'Dave Brubeck, teaching audiences to clap in 11/4 time' and 'the killer-diller mechanics of Benny Goodman'.

He has an instinctive sympathy for all musicians, even those whose work he doesn't much like. When he says of the avant-garde: 'one faces the question of how far society should pay an artist for doing something society doesn't want doing' he is gazing, unblinkingly and with no glib solution, at a problem that confronts all those who are impelled to paint the pictures, sing the songs, tell the tales or play the blues.

Throughout these pieces he juggles the personal – even the insular – with the universal. He never reviewed, and rarely attended, public performances. He is the ultimate jazz freak, alone in his room, tapping his foot and snapping his fingers to the music he loves. We all have such a room. But we also understand that we are a tiny part of the most democratic art form of the twentieth century. Anybody can join in, at least as a listener, or even as a player, given high talent and obsessive dedication. It is no coincidence that repressive regimes the world over, taking their cue from Hitler, have always hated jazz, the music that doesn't play by the rules, or as Philip describes it: 'that incredible argot that in the first half of the 20th century spoke to all nations and all intelligences equally'.

You can't beat that for a resounding yes.

Alan Plater

To the memory of Michael Bowen

Introduction

'THE NATURAL NOISE OF GOOD': PHILIP LARKIN, JAZZ JOURNALIST

*Did that make it a simplified world? Perhaps, but that hardly mattered beside
the existence of a moral seriousness that could be made apparent without the aid
of evangelical puffing and blowing.*
Kingsley Amis, *I Like It Here*

They show us what we have as it once was.
Philip Larkin, 'Reference Back'

I don't go for dumb guys.
Eddie Prue in Raymond Chandler's *The High Window*

In the Foreword to his collection of book reviews and critical essays,
Required Writing (1983), Philip Larkin observed wryly that 'it is an expected
consequence of becoming known as a writer that you are assumed to be
competent to assess other writers'. He then offered a characterisation of
the 'good reviewer' as someone who 'combines the knowledge of the
scholar with the judgment and cogency of the critic and the readability of
the journalist'—and reflected that 'knowing how far I fell short of this ideal
made me all the more laboriously anxious to do the best I could'.
Reviewers less talented—and less honest—than Larkin might welcome his
comment that 'I found reading the books hard, thinking of something to
say about them hard, and saying it hardest of all'. They might also nod
assent to his admission that 'I rarely accepted a literary assignment without
a sinking of the heart, nor finished it without a sense of relief', and endorse

the reflection that 'to undertake such commissions no doubt exercised part of my mind that would otherwise have remained dormant, and to this extent they probably did me no harm'.[1]

Although *Required Writing* was well received, Larkin wrote that on reading the proofs of these *Miscellaneous Pieces*—and 'without being falsely modest'—he had found them 'rather dull' and identified the problem: 'my trouble is that I have only two ideas or so to rub together, and when they are rubbed together remorselessly for about 150pp, the reader gets restive. Some of the reviews weren't bad. The jazz scraps at the end are a mistake.'[2]

These 'jazz scraps' included his famous or notorious Introduction to *All What Jazz*, an incisive essay on New Orleans clarinettist George Lewis, reflections on 'the excessive volatility of the jazz record world', and a statement of 'Larkin's Law of Reissues'—which posits:

> anything you haven't got already probably isn't worth bothering with. In other words, if someone tries to persuade you to buy a limited edition of the 1924–25 sessions by Paraffin Joe and his Nitelites, keep your pockets buttoned up; if they were any good, you'd have heard them at school, as you did King Oliver, and have laid out your earliest pocket money on them.[3]

A review of some recent Count Basie records was prefaced by the statement that:

> The golden rule in any art is: once you have made your name, keep in there punching. For the public is not so much endlessly gullible as endlessly hopeful; after twenty years, after forty years even, it still half expects your next book or film or play to reproduce that first fine careless rapture, however clearly you have demonstrated that whatever talent you once possessed has long since degenerated into repetition, platitude, or frivolity.[4]

More (or less) seriously, Larkin's obituary notice of Louis Armstrong—'the deep river into which flowed all the tributaries of jazz'—concluded with the reflection that

> In the great ironical takeover of western popular music by the American Negro (and remember the saying 'Let me write a nation's songs, and anyone you like may write its laws'), Armstrong stands with Ellington and Waller as one of the Trojan horses that brought it about.[5]

The profound satisfaction evident in that last perception explains why Larkin chose—despite the reservations noted above—to include pieces on jazz in a volume heavily weighted towards literary figures. Even a cursory perusal of the *Selected Letters* shows that the one area of his professional activity that Larkin never complained about or looked on with anything other than pleasure was his jazz work, and that furnishes a clue (for those who might need one) to the fact that this music was part of his *identity* and personality. As a youth in Coventry in the 1930s, he had first listened on the radio (and responded) to British dance bands like Harry Roy's, eagerly awaiting a 'hot' break from a sideman. At the local Hippodrome, he was entranced by the antics (and paraphernalia) of the resident drummer, and persuaded his parents to buy him 'an elementary drum kit and a set of tuition records by Max Abrams', on which he 'battered away contentedly, spending less time on the rudiments than in improvising an accompaniment to records'. As he recalled: 'I was, in essence, hooked on jazz even before I heard any . . . what got me was the rhythm. That simple trick of the suspended beat, that had made the slaves shuffle in Congo Square on Saturday nights, was something that never palled.' Later, with his friend Jim Sutton, Larkin remembered that

> we took it in turn to wind the portable HMV, and those white and coloured Americans, Bubber Miley, Frank Teschemacher, J. C. Higginbotham, spoke immediately to our understanding. Their rips, slurs and distortions were something we understood perfectly. This was something we had found for ourselves, that wasn't taught at school . . . There was nothing odd about this. It was happening to boys all over Europe and America. It just didn't get into the papers.[6]

In an Introduction (1963) to his first novel, *Jill* (1946), Larkin relates how this love of jazz was further stimulated by meeting Kingsley Amis at Oxford, where

> I suppose we devoted to some hundred records that early anatomizing passion normally reserved for the more established arts. 'It's the *abject entreaty* of that second phrase . . . ' 'What she's actually singing is *ick-sart-mean* . . . ' 'Isn't it marvellous the way Russell . . . ' Russell, Charles Ellsworth 'Pee Wee' (b. 1906), clarinet and saxophone player extraordinary, was, *mutatis mutandis*, our Swinburne and our Byron. We bought every record he played on that we could find, and—literally—dreamed about similar items on the American Commodore label.[7]

Yet, as Trevor Tolley has noted, studies of Larkin have tended to ignore or pay only scant attention to his undergraduate views (and later writings) on jazz—conveniently ignoring the fact that he once declared: 'I can live a week without poetry but not a day without jazz.'[8] Tolley—who devotes one chapter of *My Proper Ground: A Study of the Work of Philip Larkin and Its*

Development to *All What Jazz*—concedes that many Larkin critics and devotees might well lack 'the special knowledge needed to make a detailed judgement' of what he wrote about jazz, but adds pertinently: 'were he, like Betjeman, to have written about architecture, his views would be discussed without any condescension to the reader, whose lack of knowledge would be regarded as ignorance'. Yet Larkin did write—extensively and pertinently—about jazz and, even in a short review of Duke Ellington's career, revealed 'a power to project a new conception of an artist and to sustain it through a reordering of our perception of the whole body of his work'.

Larkin's lifelong devotion to jazz is, Tolley concludes, 'an insistence of main importance, coming from a writer of his stature' who fervently believed that 'jazz is not only a major cultural phenomenon of our time, but an art that is to be taken as seriously as any other'.[9] Not only do we share this conviction but we also believe that in his reviews of jazz literature, as in his record reviews, Larkin revealed his real (rather than imputed) attitudes to a range of 'political' and emotive issues: the experiences and aspirations of African-Americans, the tribulations and achievements of jazz women in a male-dominated society, the joys (and dangers) of alcohol, sex, and illegal substances. Furthermore, these book reviews give the lie to the charges of misogynist, racist and anti-modernist curmudgeon levelled against Larkin by politically correct critics who also reveal themselves as incapable of detecting irony or wit in the purple prose that vivifies much of his correspondence.[10]

Those charges may seem—indeed are—absurdly surreal, but even Larkin's admirers have been troubled by them. Some of the 'revelations' offered by the *Selected Letters* prompted Joseph Epstein to remark: 'I wish Larkin had never said such things because they can only be used against him by people who along with being impressed with their own virtue cannot stand too much complication in human character.'[11] Martin Amis made essentially the same point, albeit much more bullishly, when selecting his 'Books of the Year' in 1992: 'I found the humour and melancholy of Larkin's *Selected Letters* entirely addictive. Those hostile to the book betray their own amnesiac modernity. They probably know what a letter is; but they don't know what a *correspondence* is, with its intimacies and its willing suspension of accountability.'[12]

One can extend such advocacy by pointing to Larkin's masterly use of *register*. Whatever the task or occasion, his choice of diction and tone was as meticulous as varied, and nowhere is this more evident than in his reflections on jazz. Throughout his life, delightfully 'Larkinesque' aperçus peppered his notes and letters to like-minded friends. Writing from Oxford in 1941, he informed fellow-enthusiast Jim Sutton:

> I rushed out on Monday and bought 'Nobody Knows the Way I Feel This Morning'. Fucking, cunting, bloody good! Bechet is a great artist. As soon as he starts playing you automatically stop thinking about anything else and listen. Power and glory![13]

Other communications to Sutton contained the intelligence:

> Pause to play 'Harlem Air Shaft' and 'Sepia Panorama' (Ellington) that I've borrowed. They aren't so abysmal as you'd think ... Certainly Barney Bigard is shitty, but Rex Stewart blows some batty stuff & there's a fucking good rhythm section centred on Jimmy Blanton and Sonny Greer;
>
> The Chicagoans are the only gang that play jazz as white people should ... Chicago style is jazz sarcasm ... I should say that the Chicagoans are more intelligent, more 'artists' than [Red] Nichols or Bix [Bei-derbecke]. They don't stuff themselves with shit about beauty (Bix: 'Gee, ain't Louis wonderful?' [Eddie] Condon: 'Aw, go stuff yourself wid shit!'); they are conscious of a certain self-contempt.[14]

Larkin's Oxford classmate Norman Isles was asked (in 1963): 'Do you remember burbling "My wife revolves a barrel" against Armstrong's *Body and Soul* in Kingsley's room? This was your mishearing of "My life revolves around her." '[15] Amis himself was once informed that it is

> Just past midnight, a dull cold day (yes, why is it so fucking *cold?* April, innit?) which I have largely spent in taping the 1923 Olivers to see if they sound better. Don't know that they do. A record I bought recently is 'The Individualism of Pee Wee Russell' ... Don't get excited, but I wonder if you know it:—'live' recordings with [Ruby] Braff and some nondescript buggers, Boston 1952, just after his near-fatal illness.[16]

It was Larkin's own idea to collect and publish his *Daily Telegraph* jazz record reviews. When Faber & Faber's sales director asked him to suggest some publicity angles that would promote the book, Larkin furnished the requisite information: 'I became a jazz addict at the age of 12 or 13, listened avidly to all the dance bands of the day and tried to learn to play the drums, began collecting records, and although far from being an expert, have never ceased to be an enthusiast'. He advised Faber to think of *All What Jazz* as a 'freak publication' and 'not as a piece of jazz scholarship or even as any sort of contribution to the field'. Rather, he suggested, Faber should 'treat it like a book by T. S. Eliot on all-in wrestling'.[17]

All What Jazz was dedicated to Donald Mitchell, who had initially suggested Larkin as jazz critic for the paper. As he informed Mitchell in 1968: 'This job, despite the peevishness of some of the articles, has brought me a great deal of pleasure, and I hope to go on with it.'[18] In a Footnote to the second edition, Larkin suggested that 'listening to new jazz records for an hour with a pint of gin and tonic is the best remedy for a day's work I know'. His critics notwithstanding, Larkin claimed that

> I still love jazz: the great coloured pioneers and their eager white disciples, and the increasingly remote world that surrounded their music, dance halls, derby hats, band buses, tuxedos, monogrammed music stands, the shabby recording studios where they assembled, and the hanging honeycomb microphones that saved it all for us.[19]

Not included in the text of *Jazz Writings* but certainly worth mentioning here are Larkin's reflections on jazz, written a year before his death, in response to (unsolicited) queries from the music critic and broadcaster Steve Race. A professed admirer of Larkin's poetry, *All What Jazz* and *Required Writing*, Race was perplexed 'that so persuasive a propagandist for literature should have ears so firmly closed when it came to developments in music' (i.e. jazz). More precisely, Race wondered why, for Larkin, 'jazz has to be instantly accessible', and 'if it doesn't grab you from the start, it's pretentious nonsense'. Larkin's reply to this query was a considered restatement of his aesthetic credo and deserves extended quotation:

> My objection to modern jazz is not that it is pretentious, but simply that it isn't anything like the jazz I loved and began collecting. I must emphasise that I am not a music lover in any real sense of the word; it is only jazz that won my allegiance. I have no difficulty in relating to the ODJB, King Oliver, Armstrong, Bessie, Bix and the rest, down to Basie, Goodman and Bob Crosby. But there it seems to end. What comes after may be technically brilliant and racially justified, but it leaves me cold.
>
> We both like pre-Parker jazz, but you went on to enjoy the innovations of Parker and his successors and I didn't. Can this arise from the fact that you are an exceptionally gifted musician, whereas I never got beyond the FACE/EGBDF stage? I can readily imagine that modern jazz is much more fun to play if you are musically sophisticated. Unfortunately it is not much more fun to listen to if you are not musically sophisticated. You are saying that if this is the case, then I must educate myself.

What I don't believe about art is that it should require special knowledge or special training on the part of its consumers. Art is enjoyment, first on the part of the writer, painter or musician, and then, by communication, on the part of the reader and looker and listener. But the second enjoyment has to come out of the first, not out of the conscious learning of technical theory.

You have to give the audience something to enjoy, to hold on to, right from the start, and this is just what I never found in those by-now-venerable ancestors Parker, Davis and Monk, let alone in their numerous and increasingly abrasive successors. Well, perhaps that is not quite true: there are very occasional bits of them I enjoy after a fashion. But Johnny Hodges, Henry Allen and Fats Waller blow them out of the room any day of the week.

Replying to Race's subsequent query 'are your jazz tastes, as I suspect, simply nostalgia for your undergraduate days?', Larkin replied that 'I certainly think I suffered from not hearing jazz from about 1942 until 1956, starting with the Petrillo ban and stopping when I got a flat where I could make a moderate amount of noise. But when I started reviewing records in 1961 there was a lot of leeway to make up, and I don't think I ever managed it emotionally.'[20]

Those hostile to Larkin have been quick to agree. In the year following his death, jazz critic Max Harrison proclaimed that: 'By 1961 Larkin had no idea where jazz was',[21] and in his recent collection *Reading Jazz*, editor Robert Gottlieb prefaced the inclusion of the Introduction to *All What Jazz* with the dismissive, 'No one who knows Larkin's work will be surprised at his biting contempt for jazz's latest directions.'[22] And it has to be said that at times—as can be inferred from his remarks to Steve Race—Larkin hardly helped his own cause. In 1971, in the process of declining an invitation to appear on a television programme as an 'eminent authority on jazz', he wrote:

I have never been able to claim the real specialised knowledge of the record collector or the jazz historian or the musicologist. All I have . . . is an ability to write smart journalism that makes the record sound attractive or unattractive as the case may be.[23]

As Kingsley Amis observed in another context, 'That's no way to go on. [It ignores] that most elementary maxim of the writer's trade, *People take you at your own evaluation*. If you tell them you're a genius, or a mere entertainer, they'll tell one another you're a genius, or a mere entertainer'[24] (Amis's italics). Or, by extension, an inexpert smart journalist. Jazz critic Steve Voce made much the same point in his 1985 tribute:

> I was much saddened by the news of the death today (December 2) of Philip Larkin, our greatest poet and a man who wrote on the subject of jazz with great sensitivity, although he constantly belittled himself without cause. He was a far more perceptive listener than I, and I was embarrassed when he wrote to me as recently as September: 'You really mustn't think of me as someone in your league jazzwise . . . ' What nonsense![25]

Nonsense indeed. Convinced that *All What Jazz* is one of the essential works of jazz literature, we began the task of collecting the reviews, articles, reports and letters that comprise this complementary volume in the further belief that Larkin was a jazz critic of the first order. Unearthing the resultant 67 pieces not only occasioned an excitement analogous to that which might attend the discovery of new Larkin poems: it has had the effect of elevating that belief into something we would put forward as fact.

The most immediately striking feature of *Jazz Writings* is the sheer quality of Larkin's prose; such is its grace, wit and precise eloquence that one can confidently recommend the collection to readers whose interest in jazz is slight. In his Foreword, Alan Plater draws attention to instances of 'a poet at work', and there are many others:

> (He) rounds it all off by asking if jazz and classical music can't get together. I should say this happened about ten years ago. The problem now is to get them apart. **[5]**

> I am sorry that no one saw fit to tell Ellington's reaction to Shakespeare, whom he read before writing 'Such Sweet Thunder': 'You know what? All these lines have five beats.' **[6]**

> . . . as in most pictorial music, the programme note seems irrelevant whenever the piece is successful, like scaffolding dismantled after use. **[6]**

> [Bix] Beiderbecke's ideal biographer might have been Scott Fitzgerald, who would have retained the romance of his career while recognising the tragedy of his character. **[8]**

> There are not many perfect things in jazz, but [Sidney] Bechet playing the blues could be one of them. **[12]**

> Reading *Night Creature* is like picking one's way through what seems alternatively a battlefield, an archaeological site, and a deserted museum . . . What was happy entertainment is now harsh didacticism, when it is not part of a glum college syllabus. **[45]**

> As a jazz pianist [Fats Waller] stands between James P. Johnson, who taught him, and Art Tatum, who learnt from him, but it is he who has the greatest

variety of mood, from feather-light whimsicality to the solid springing tenths in the left hand that never let the rhythm falter for a moment. **[25]**

he is aware of the opportunities for the charlatan that a revolution in any art provides, and thinks he can distinguish, so to speak, the Shepps from the goats. **[28]**

we are left in the end with an impression of brilliant superficiality. Perhaps this is editorial policy: the *New Yorker* was always strong on polish. But the only thing you can polish is a surface. **[30]**

(Bop) has been ... called development. But there are different kinds of development: a hot bath can develop into a cold one. **[49]**

These ten extracts, chosen freely if not quite at random, do not just demonstrate felicity of style. They combine an unerring ear and eye with exactitude of judgment, dramatising a natural and easy authority: *'he knows what he is talking about'*.[26]

Larkin is on principle a generous critic, seeking to dispense praise where possible, express antipathy where necessary and above all to persuade the reader to investigate the source works anew. In 1966 he wrote

[A critic] must hold on to the principle that the only reason for praising a work is that it pleases and the way to develop his critical sense is to be more acutely aware of whether he is being pleased or not.[27]

The accent on the pleasure principle is crucial, but it is not exclusive. A later observation both complements and sternly amplifies that earlier definition:

a critic, after all, is a man who likes some things and dislikes others, and finds reasons for doing so and for trying to persuade other people to do so. (1981; **[45]**)

It is no accident that this remark is made while assessing the work of Whitney Balliett. Larkin has an immense admiration for the *New Yorker* columnist's style—'Balliett ... brings jazz journalism to the verge of poetry', he once enthused[28]—and on one level he welcomes his 'hospitality of taste' as 'highly pleasing ... in an age where "criticism" has come to mean "adverse criticism" '.[29] At the same time, he is nagged with dissatisfaction, finding suspect Balliett's refusal to offer anything in the way of discriminating judgment or indeed personal preference. In the same piece he notes

> None of the complimentary remarks about Balliett and his other books
> reproduced on the jacket of this one uses the word 'critic', and that may well be
> significant . . . [since criticism] is alien to Balliett's purpose.

This articulates—even more starkly—reservations expressed earlier:

> His chief characteristic, as a critic, is that he has virtually no characteristics: in a
> potted biography published in 1959 it was said that Balliett 'professes equal
> interest in all types of jazz'. **[30]**

The four reviews of Balliett's work collected here pay due tribute to his gifts
of portraiture and 'being there' evocation, but there is a finality of
judgment in each: Larkin had little time for people who 'like everything'.

On the other hand, he had still less time for bad writing or shoddy work,
and he is remorseless in exposing ignorance and cant. And so Barry Ulanov
[5] is implicitly advised to stick to jazz rather than meddle with things
beyond his ken;[30] two chroniclers of his beloved Bix Beiderbecke mete out
'sesquipedalian agony,' not least through their rendering of 'later' as
'posterior in date to' **[8]**; a critic with 'a real feeling for jazz' is nonetheless
branded as 'a shocking writer', at once 'intolerably long-winded', cursed
with a mind which 'wanders all over the place' and (most damning of all)
'facetious' **[14]**.

Just occasionally, too, there is anger. In the main this takes the form of
generalised rage on behalf of African-Americans, but it can become
personal, as occurs during his appraisal of James Lincoln Collier's book on
Louis Armstrong, one of his last reviews. After a number of soberly
agnostic paragraphs, Larkin suddenly erupts: 'This is all profoundly
depressing, the depressingness of the half truth. What does Collier expect
Armstrong to have done about [the circumstances that limited him]? Turn
himself into Miles Davis? Put the Negro question forward 50 years?' It is
not just that Larkin's greatest hero is being belittled: the anger is chiefly at
the author's lordly ignorance and his failure to provide any sense of
'Armstrong himself' or of his charisma as 'a great artist, a great personality,
a great human being'. Those words have a passion that removes any
danger of mawkishness, additionally supported by the unanswerable
dismissal: 'For that matter, can any depressing book about Armstrong be
more than half true?'

What most distinguishes the criticism housed in *Jazz Writings*, therefore,
is a respect for and pleasure in jazz writing that is informed, intelligent and
unafraid to offer judgment and preference. Larkin is full of praise for

Marshall Stearns, Benny Green and Barry McRae while making it clear that he begs to differ with the conclusions they draw—in McRae's case, spectacularly so. The same applies, *mutatis mutandis*, to his approbation for Francis Newton and Paul Oliver, even though Newton 'has little charm as a writer' and Oliver's prose is 'somewhat colourless'. Moreover, these and the other writers he lauds most have heart and brain in the right place: it is the music *as music* that matters first and foremost. Conversely, the polemic of LeRoi Jones's *Blues People* renders it 'a work of sociology rather than music criticism', and Charles Keil's 1966 attempt to argue that contemporary blues is more dignified and racially relevant than its earlier counterparts receives even shorter shrift, via the magisterial

> all the sociological justification in the world isn't going to make the 'refined' blues that is the speciality of this mode ... any more impressive as jazz music.

Some might find gratuitous the semi-malevolent glee with which Larkin punctures their pretension,[31] but two things should be said in his defence. First, history has vindicated him in both instances. *Blues People* (recently reprinted) suffers from Jones's hugely inflated appraisal of the 'New Thing',[32] whereas Keil's book has simply sunk without trace. Second, neither writer offers any valuable insight into the recordings at issue, and for the most part one's own aural experience is wildly at odds with what they purport to hear and what they claim for it. And that leads us neatly to jazz on record.

In this particular respect *All What Jazz* and *Jazz Writings* would seem to be not so much complementary as opposites. The former, as its subtitle *A Record Diary* indicates, is devoted almost entirely to recordings—over 900 of them, in fact—whereas this collection does not contain a single record review *per se*. Yet recorded jazz is a central issue throughout *Jazz Writings*; indeed, there are grounds for arguing that it is addressed here with greater conceptual vigour and authority of context than in its companion *All What Jazz*. For in *All What Jazz*, after all, Larkin's business was the monthly, more or less on-the-spot assessment of the latest issues and reissues. Only at the very end—when he was evidently tiring of the work and deeply depressed about the state of jazz—did he fail to do this surpassingly well, but in a precise sense his horizons were limited, dependent on which records were sent him (and which were not).

In the pieces that make up *Jazz Writings*, however, he is afforded many opportunities to reflect on jazz's future and the importance of recordings in its prospects of survival. In the 1982 interview conducted for *Paris Review* he reflected: 'Anyway, [jazz is] dead now, dead as Elizabethan madrigal singing. We can only treasure the records. And I do.'[33] Almost exactly the same sentiments are to be found here in his fond recollection of the 1937–39 Count Basie sides made for Decca (see **[2]**), the final sentence of the 1963 piece on Charlie Parker **[20]**, the remarkably upbeat conclusion to his 1971 obituary on Armstrong and the 1974 essay on Beiderbecke: 'Only the indestructible delight of his records remains.'

Even more eloquent are his wholehearted endorsement of Derek Langridge's assertion **[53]** that: 'The real jazz lover must be a record collector' and his 1961–70 'Record of the Year' choices for the *Daily Telegraph* **[57–66]**. As Alan Plater observes in his Foreword—and it is a point which only the late Derek Jewell has made before[34]—Larkin never reviewed a jazz gig and for that matter hardly ever attended one. Now to a certain kind of jazz enthusiast, 'being there' is almost everything: jazz in the living room cannot begin to compete with jazz in the club, the concert hall or (these days especially) the festival complex; moreover, many jazz musicians are quick to tell you how much more stimulating it is to play a live concert than to attempt top-flight creativity in the cold confines of the studio. Larkin would have understood what they—fan and practitioner alike—were talking about, but he would never have agreed. He would undoubtedly have welcomed the CD revolution that gathered full momentum shortly after his death and which has been responsible for restoring so much near-forgotten jazz to widespread circulation; he would have been no less delighted by the consequent and new enthusiasm for jazz amongst the young. But such cheering technological advances would only have confirmed him in his belief that what will survive of jazz is—literally—a matter of record.

And that is why the apparent ephemera preserved in **57–66** are so significant. They ought by rights to be museum pieces, of interest only to 'anoraked enthusiasts', in Alan Plater's charming phrase. But as he—and we[35]—note, over a generation later Larkin's choices could be embraced wholesale by any new enthusiast in search of a core collection, or indeed by any *aficionado* who might be asked to explain why recorded jazz is important and why it might still matter a century from now.

Moreover, those choices illuminate (in some ways almost 'correct') the initial judgments contained in *All What Jazz*. His 1961 comment on Cannonball Adderley: 'It has been [his] year here, and this disc exhibits his full-throated alto more undilutedly than any', is decisively warmer than the original review; the same goes for his nomination of Art Tatum and Ben Webster in 1965 and for that year's (amazing) citation of John Coltrane's *A Love Supreme*,[36] described with no trace of rancour or irony as 'a four-part attempt by the sheets-of-sound father of the New Thing to say "Thank You, God" in his own angular fashion, moving from frenzy to faith in doing so'.

No less noteworthy, both as choices and in their phrasing, are two of his 1968 selections: Thelonious Monk's 'gay and fruitful piano' and the 'bleak pastoralism delivered with a melancholy and kingly authority' that he honours in his supposed *bête noire*, Miles Davis. But the most surprising appearance is that of Ornette Coleman in 1967. Larkin's readers at the time might have been even more astonished than we are, since the original review was never published: it was written for the August column that chiefly comprised what was, in effect, an obituary of John Coltrane which the proprietors presumably considered too controversial to print. None of that can diminish the warmth and accuracy of his judgment of 'this philosophic free-former': *Chappaqua Suite* dramatises 'his consistency of conception and inventiveness without recourse to distortion'.

The fact that Larkin took with complete seriousness his duties as annual pollster is not just a tribute to his consummate professionalism. As is by now evident, jazz records *mattered* to him—and more rather than less as the years went by. The 1967 selection that includes the 'Coleman bomb-shell' opens with the sentence 'As reissue programmes grow, today's players have increasingly to struggle against the giants of the 'Thirties and even their own younger selves', an observation combining elegy and celebration in equal amounts. If 'The jazz that conquered the world . . . is dying with its practitioners', as he remarked three years later,[37] that made it all the more vital that what it achieved during its life be unfailingly preserved, available to all.

There will doubtless be those who persist for a while in viewing Larkin as a racist, as someone who disliked eighty per cent of jazz music, or even both. However, *Jazz Writings* demonstrates that they are going to have a harder time of it in future.

For its pages are not so much sprinkled with as drenched in admiring sympathy for African-Americans in general and the jazz artist—black and white—in particular. What appears to be his very first jazz piece (see **67**) may be clumsily written and pretentious at times, but its tenor is the very opposite of racist and, furthermore, it is anything but reactionary, hailing jazz as a 'new art' and as the quintessence of American music—audacious claims in 1940. And that championing idealism never left him, even when bop and its aftermath moved jazz in directions which he did not care for. The whole of the review of Ralph Ellison's *Shadow and Act* testifies to it, and a 1971 echo of the 'Trojan horse' observation[38] puts the calumnists even more firmly in their place: 'While we are wondering whether to integrate with Africa, Armstrong (and Ellington, and Waller, and all the countless others) has done it behind our backs' **[35]**. Similarly, the contention, 'What was so exciting about jazz was the way its unique, simple gaiety communicated itself to such widely differing kinds of human being' **[18]**, may seem a touch sentimental to some, but could never strike anyone as the work of a bigot, who would not even have such thoughts, let alone publish them abroad.

Time and again, too, he wonders—with a kind of enchanted bewilderment—how a music founded in and expressive of the miserable abominations of slavery could take over the globe. One such instance occurs at the beginning of his review of *The Jazz Scene* and finds Larkin equalling the author, fellow-Companion of Honour Eric Hobsbawm, in both musical and historical authority:

> One cannot consider jazz without being astonished at the speed with which it has gained ascendancy over popular musical taste in societies and cultures very different from that which produced it. Indeed, there is a curious logic in the world's enthusiastic response to the music of the Negro, as if in some gigantic Jungian case-history where salvation is shown to lie in whatever is most feared and despised. **[10]**

But while he is stirringly anxious to portray jazz and its practitioners as heroic, Larkin is simultaneously aware that it is no less a *tragic* art. Full of admiration for the jazzman as 'the twentieth century's version of the traditional artist' **[2]**, Larkin is 'struck by certain recurrent features' **[15]**—a cycle of rapid recognition, intense practice, refusal to compromise and then, too often, collapse or betrayal.

> The lives of early jazzmen were often peculiarly hard. Unable to see their art outside a world where harsh exploitation was the rule, they were also at the mercy of the American economic climate and the fashions of show business. When their strength and originality left them, too often they returned to a miserable and obscure poverty, with nothing remaining of their work but a few recordings on a soon-defunct label. **[4]**

A similar pattern characterises the more obviously self-destructive experience of many of the modernists, especially Parker and Billie Holiday.

Indeed, in *Requiem For Jazz* **[49]**, arguably the most distinguished piece in this entire collection, Larkin equates Parker's apparent death-wish with the self-immolation of jazz itself, and the lines of Wordsworth's that he quotes while reflecting on Django Reinhardt:

> We poets in our youth began in gladness,
> But thereof come in the end despondency and madness

have an epigraphic force: that, in several significant respects, is how he perceives jazz history as a whole.

To close on such a sombre note would not, however, be appropriate. For quite apart from the constant delights of Larkin's prose, these pieces abound in affirmation. They celebrate many fine studies (whose importance may now be newly appreciated) as much as Larkin's own pleasure and scholarly mastery. On a personal note, we wish to celebrate the unearthing of 'historical material whose value is increased by the fugitive nature of the originals'; the words are Larkin's, from one of the rarer items collected here (the article for *Tempo* **[19]**), but they almost uncannily describe the excitement we felt at such discoveries. This collection fills a lacuna in the Larkin *oeuvre*, and demonstrates that as a jazz book reviewer he triumphantly fulfilled the mandate announced in *Required Writing*. Individually and collectively, these sixty-seven pieces combine 'the knowledge of the scholar with the judgment and cogency of the critic and the readability of the journalist'. Indeed, they do even more than that. On several occasions Larkin pleaded for 'a *belle-lettriste* of jazz, a Newman or Cardus'; the pages which follow show that jazz had one all along.

Richard Palmer
John White
Hull, January 1999

Notes

1 Philip Larkin, *Required Writing: Miscellaneous Pieces 1955–1982* (London: Faber & Faber, 1983).

2 To Anthony Thwaite, 14 August 1983 in Anthony Thwaite, ed., *Selected Letters of Philip Larkin, 1940–1985* (London: Faber & Faber, 1992), 701–2.

3 *Required Writing*, 305.

4 Ibid. 306.

5 Ibid. 314–15. Asked by Faber for his opinion on commissioning a book on Armstrong, Larkin wrote to Charles Monteith in 1971: 'It is already accepted—or if it isn't, it soon will be—that Louis Armstrong was an enormously important cultural figure in our century, more important than Picasso in my opinion, but certainly quite comparable.' He also offered the suggestion that such a study 'might be a cultural work, taking Armstrong as a kind of Trojan horse of Negro values sent into white civilisation under the cover of entertainment'. Larkin to Charles Monteith: 3 August 1971: *Selected Letters*, 443, 444.

6 Philip Larkin, *All What Jazz: A Record Diary 1961–1971* (London: Faber & Faber, 1970), 16. Asked by Miriam Gross, during an *Observer* interview in 1979, how he first became interested in jazz, Larkin replied: 'It started as soon as I heard anything with four beats to the bar, which was, in my early days, dance music. Jack Payne, Billy Cotton, Harry Roy. I listened to bands like that for an awfully long time without realizing that there was such a thing as American jazz . . . I always think of Ray Noble's "Tiger Rag" as my first jazz record: not really very jazzy but it was a jazz number; and the second one I bought was the Washboard Rhythm Kings' "I'm gonna play down by the Ohio", which I've still got. And the third was Louis Armstrong's "Ain't Misbehavin" '. Of course once I'd got that the way was clear.' *Required Writing*, 50.

7 Philip Larkin, *Jill* (London: Faber & Faber, 1975), 17. Larkin relates that along with his fellow enthusiasts at Oxford, 'jazz became part of the private joke of existence, rather than a public expertise: expressions such as "combined pimp and lover" and "eating the cheaper cuts of pork" (both from a glossary on *Yellow Dog Blues*) flecked our conversations cryptically; for some reason, [Max] Kaminsky's plaintive little introduction to "Home Cooking" became a common signal, and any of us entering the steam-filled college bath-house would whistle it to see if it was taken up from behind any of the bolted partition doors.' *All What Jazz*, 17. Amis recalled of this period that: 'With Philip the music [jazz] was a preoccupation, a passion, as it was for numbers of his and our friends and as it soon became for me . . . our heroes were the white Chicagoans, Count Basie's band, Bix Beiderbecke, Sidney Bechet, Henry Allen, Muggsy Spanier, Fats Waller, early Armstrong and early Ellington . . . and our heroines Bessie Smith, Billie Holiday, Rosetta Howard . . . and Cleo Brown. All gone now.' Kingsley Amis, *Memoirs* (London: Hutchinson, 1991), 52.

8 'Poet on the 8.15': interview with Philip Larkin by J. Horder, *Guardian*, 20 May 1965, 9.

9 T. Tolley, *My Proper Ground: A Study of the Work of Philip Larkin and Its Development* (Edinburgh University Press, 1991), 137, 139. Tolley observes that 'Larkin's tastes in jazz should be seen . . . in their historical perspective. Interest in jazz in England began with the collecting of the hotter dance music records of the twenties . . . The new "swing" music that emerged in America with the triumph of Benny Goodman's Orchestra in 1935 was not as well received by many British jazz collectors as it was by the young Larkin, some of whom regarded it as a commercialization of jazz.' *Ibid.* 145.

10 See Donald Mitchell, 'Larkin's Music', in Anthony Thwaite, ed., *Larkin at Sixty* (London: Faber & Faber, 1982), 75–8, and John White, ' "Goodbye Witherspoon": a Jazz Friendship', in Dale Salwak, ed., *Philip Larkin: The Man and His Work* (London: Macmillan, 1989), 38–47.

11 Joseph Epstein, 'Mr Larkin Gets A Life', *Life Stories* (New York: Norton, 1997), 252. Reprinted in *About Larkin: The Newsletter of the Philip Larkin Society*, 5 (April 1998), 10–15.

12 *Independent on Sunday* magazine, 29 November 1992.

13 Andrew Motion, *Philip Larkin: A Writer's Life* (London: Faber & Faber, 1993), 47.

14 To J. B. Sutton, 23 June 1941: *Selected Letters*, 15–16; to J. B. Sutton, 16 February 1941, *Ibid.* 20–1.

15 To Norman Isles, 25 January, 1963: *Ibid.* 349.

16 To Kingsley Amis, 26 April 1980: *Ibid.* 618.

17 To Peter Crawley, 19 June 1969: *Ibid.* 416. Larkin advised Anthony Thwaite of the imminent appearance of *All What Jazz*: 'Try to imagine a book by

Humphrey Lyttelton saying that modern poetry is no good, while at the same time charmingly admitting he's never read any since 1940, and you will get some idea of how mine will be handled.' *Ibid.* 425.

18 Larkin to Donald Mitchell, 20 November 1968: *Ibid.* 408.

19 *All What Jazz*, 29, 31.

20 'Dear Mr Larkin', *The Sunday Telegraph Review*, 18 November 1990, 1. See Larkin's review of Race's autobiography, *Musician at Large* **[43]**.

21 Max Harrison, 'The Pleasures of Ignorance', *Wire*, 34/35 (December 1986 and January 1987), 61. At one point Harrison adds that Larkin's 'assertion that the listener's "ear will tell him instantly whether a piece of music is vital, musical, exciting, or cerebral, mock-academic, dead" is . . . quite simply a lie'. Just what makes Harrison able to alchemise a statement about personal aural experience into proof of determined mendacity is a mystery.

22 Robert Gottlieb, ed., *Reading Jazz* (London: Bloomsbury, 1997), 798. Gottlieb's competence as a commentator on Larkin may be further gauged by his citing of Larkin's book as *All What Jazz? (sic)*.

23 See **[54]** below.

24 Kingsley Amis, *The James Bond Dossier* (London: Panther, 1966), 141.

25 Steve Voce, 'It Don't Mean A Thing', *Jazz Journal International* xxix/1 (1986), 9.

26 Larkin on Humphrey Lyttelton (see **[6]** below). The italics are Larkin's; the most dignified of stylists, he kept typographical emphases to a minimum, and any such instance would therefore seem to signal something of unusual importance to him. That is certainly the case here.

27 *All What Jazz*, 156.

28 *Ibid.* 212.

29 See **[21]** below.

30 Larkin notes Ulanov's inclusion of 'one of those charts that show what has happened in jazz and the arts since 1900' and further observes that it suggests that 'nothing has happened in literature since 1949 except something called "The Cypresses Believe in God".'

31 Further instances include Larkin's withering parting shot at Keil's prose —'where even bowling with the boys has "the non-avocational aspect of increasing group solidarity" '—and his judgment that 'the despairing aggression' of Jones's work 'does not make for comfortable reading. Nor, I'm afraid, does it make for literature without other qualities of originality and organisation Mr Jones does not seem to possess at the moment.'

32 Notwithstanding our own reservations about Jones as jazz critic and Larkin's remarks quoted in Note 31 above, it should be pointed out that Jones—more recently known as Amiri Baraka—is much admired in some circles as a poet, dramatist and short story writer. And, as John Osborne (Secretary of the Philip Larkin Society and literary critic) adds: 'One might therefore claim that the

chief interest of his *Blues People* is as an adjunct to his own literary work—in much the same way that many people will read *All What Jazz* and *Larkin's Jazz* [Jazz Writings] for what they tell us about the formation of Larkin the poet.'

33 *Required Writing*, 72.
34 See Note 12 to Part Two below.
35 See below, page 162.
36 The original reviews in *All What Jazz* are on pages 48 (Adderley), 144–5 (Tatum & Webster) and 142 (Coltrane).
37 *All What Jazz*, 261.
38 See Note 5 above.

I sincerely believe that the best criticism is that which is both amusing and poetic: not a cold, mathematical criticism which, on the pretext of explaining everything, has neither love nor hate, and voluntarily strips itself of every shred of temperament . . . To be just, that is to say, to justify its existence, criticism should be partial, passionate and political, that is to say, written from an exclusive point of view, but a point of view that opens up the widest horizons.

Charles Baudelaire

Prelude

On Wednesday evening in A1 [*a university room*] Philip Larkin made his first appearance as a guest speaker for a union society. At an English Society function, Mr. Larkin gave not a talk on the poet as librarian, but instead an introduction to a jazz recital.

The knowledge that Mr. Larkin writes occasionally for both the *Daily Telegraph* and the *Observer* on jazz led a large audience to suppose this meeting would be a valuable experience; it was also an extremely entertaining event.

This, one would expect, would meet with Mr. Larkin's favour, for he deeply feels that jazz is to be appreciated not as a musical exercise in technique but as an emotional experience, one that can exhilarate or sadden. He expressly referred to the capability of jazz to encourage comradeship.

The recital was largely a skeleton outline of jazz development cleverly condensed and constructed. It is an impossible task to reduce jazz with its rich development to the playing of thirteen tracks from various records. Mr. Larkin met this task by charmingly relating jazz history to his own experiences of it. Amongst the Adderley, Parker, Gillespie, Ellington, Armstrong, Lewis and Coltrane, we therefore had Fats Waller, Josh White and Harry Roy.[1]

Mr. Larkin felt that jazz oscillated between two poles. One being the communal, exciting chant of church music, illustrated by the Reverend

Kelsey's congregation in Memphis and which now Brookmeyer and McCann look back at with varying degrees of success in their search for 'funky' or 'soul' music. 'Funky,' it is interesting to reflect, in an earlier period meant 'obnoxious' or 'smelly'.

The other pole is that of the individual meditative blues, illustrated by John Lee Hooker playing finger-style guitar and singing 'Church Bell Tollin',' and including not only country blues singers but the great Billie Holiday.

It was clear that Mr. Larkin's main sympathies lie with the jazz of the decade preceding the bop era. It was therefore very surprising that though we heard Lester Young, Basie and Ellington, no Whiteman or Goldkette bands featuring Bix Beiderbecke, and no Fletcher Henderson orchestra were featured. It is to be hoped that Mr. Larkin will have the opportunity and will agree to expand more fully on this period in future meetings, and to demonstrate the catholic interests he has in jazz, a characteristic too rare in the sharply categorised world of the jazz critic today.[2]

Anon., *Torchlight 69* (23 October 1962)

This piece was a report of a University of Hull English Society meeting and was published in the university's then house journal.

Notes

1 The range of examples reported is notable, given Larkin's known tastes (referred to at the end of the piece). To offer a lay audience as broadly representative an outline as he could within the time may seem an unexceptional achievement, but it points both to his professionalism and his erudition—qualities which have not always been recognised in his work as a jazz critic.

2 The anonymous writer's conclusion is as intriguing as warm. By this time Larkin had spent nearly two years as the *Daily Telegraph*'s jazz correspondent, and 'catholic' is not an adjective that many jazz fans would have applied to his judgments. Nevertheless, it is a judicious choice, as both *All What Jazz* and the current text demonstrate beneath their polemic. In addition, the writer is astute in drawing attention to the 'sharply categorised' world of jazz criticism—then and now—and persuasive in his implication that Larkin was much more reliable in his assessments across the spectrum than many of his colleagues.

PART ONE

Reviews in Newspapers and Periodicals

1

The Mighty Mezz

REALLY THE BLUES by Milton 'Mezz' Mezzrow and Bernard Wolfe (Secker &
Warburg, 25s)

Chicagoan Mezz Mezzrow, born of Russian-Jewish parents in 1899, was
one of that first generation of northern whites to be hit between the ears
by the jazz of New Orleans' emigrants in the early twenties. As unhesitat-
ingly as the rest, he made it his life's business. Unlike the rest, however, he
was not content with adopting the Negro's music: he wanted the whole
Negro Weltanschauung as well:

> Their wonderful music just reflected their whole make-up, their refreshing
> outlook and philosophy of living. You start out with just a technical interest in
> their music-making, but as soon as you begin analysing it you wind up trying to
> dig how they live and think and feel.

Or, as Eddie Condon says elsewhere, 'There was nothing you could do
about Mezz: when he fell through the Mason-Dixie line he just kept
going.' He progressed, therefore, from admiring the Negroes to settling
amongst them; in 1929 he moved to Harlem, took a coloured wife, and
lived through the depression by peddling marihuana. (When gaoled for
this, he registered as a Negro and ran the coloured prison orchestra.) At
intervals he organised recording groups, and in 1937, incredible as it may
seem, he headed a mixed group on Broadway until the club was closed by
its creditors. His somewhat insecure reputation as a jazz clarinettist rests
mainly on sides made with Tommy Ladnier and Sidney Bechet, and on the
writings of a certain gullible continental critic.[1] When the book ends he is

managing the *King Jazz* record company; today, I believe, he is living in Paris, out of Jim Crow's reach. It is hard not to like Mezz as Mr Wolfe presents him: he is so excitable, so grateful for a kind word, so narrow minded, so generously indignant about the mean and ugly cruelties of segregation. On the other hand, the reader should be warned that he is about as *typical* a figure as William Blake.[2] Though jazz, Negroes, and marihuana are certainly related subjects, they are not wedded to the point of synonymity, as this book suggests; and while the American Negro may well be a more attractive figure than his persecutors, Mezzrow's adulation verges on the simple-minded (his four-page imaginary conversation between himself and some other Harlem inhabitants may purport to exhibit the language of jive, but is in fact, strictly, an Empsonian pastoral).[3]

Jazz initiates, too, will wish for a post-script covering the last ten years (the book was first published in 1946), because the white New Orleans revival and the coloured invention of bop both run directly counter to Mezz's racial theories. The book, however, remains full of fascination. Anyone interested in drug addiction, the earlier jazzmen, the position of the American Negro or the torture of the English language will find it irresistible, and it will remind many a jazz-lover that his music is not so pure and abstract as his plastic-sleeved LPs seem to suggest.

Truth, 26 April 1957[4]

2
The New Bohemia

JAZZMEN edited by Frederic Ramsey, Jnr, and Charles Edward Smith (Sidgwick & Jackson, 30s)

EDDIE CONDON'S TREASURY OF JAZZ edited by Eddie Condon and Richard Gehman (Peter Davies, 30s)

COUNT BASIE AND HIS ORCHESTRA by Raymond Horricks (Gollancz, 21s)

The US publication of *Jazzmen* (in 1939, not 1946 as the Hon. Gerald Lascelles says in his 21–line introduction) inaugurated a new era of jazz appreciation. Till then, jazz writers had kept to the music, its folk-art status, use of polyphony, peculiar intonation and classical affiliations. Transcripts of famous solos and ensemble passages were appended. With *Jazzmen* the Jazz Legend burst—almost the Jazz Myth, for isn't there an underlying suggestion that New Orleans was Eden, and the 1917 closing of Storyville a kind of ancestral expulsion therefrom?[5] *Jazzmen*, with its ancient, unbelievable photographs of primal figures in band uniform or tuxedo, and a frankly biographical approach that made full use of the subjects' raffish social background, created a new *vie de Bohème*, where between commercialism and starvation the twentieth century's version of the traditional artist scrambled for a living, his status compromised at every turn by bad working conditions and racial prejudice. Anyone who doubts this need only compare the approach of Louis Armstrong's *Swing That Music* (1937) with that of his *Satchmo: My Life in New Orleans* (1951).

Nevertheless, after twenty years this collection of essays inevitably seems less impressive than it did. So much it contains has been treated at

5

length elsewhere—by Lomax and Borneman, Condon and Mezzrow, for instance, and the many voices of *Hear Me Talkin' To Ya*.[6] But its tremendous pioneering gusto remains. Frederic Ramsey's account of the rise and fall of Joe Oliver is surely a classic of its kind. In *Jazzmen*, too, so many famous remarks first received wide circulation—'Albert, I want you to learn my Boogie Woogie'; 'I wonder if we'll ever be able to play hot jazz for a living'; and of course 'After that night, they never called him anything but "King" Oliver'.

Eddie Condon's Treasury of Jazz makes an excellent follow-up to *Jazzmen*, for its first 329 pages (before the stories start) deal not only with Condon and his associates but with most of the big names made since 1930—Goodman, Waller, Basie, for instance, and even such antipathetic phenomena as Granz,[7] Parker, Kenton, Brubeck and the West Coast antique-dealers ('What does Turk Murphy do? Wrestle?'): in fact, though without any such explicit intention, it handsomely bridges the gap since 1939. Again, the approach is journalistic and anecdotal rather than scholarly, but there are good essays on Wild Bill Davison, Gillespie, and Hampton, and Goodman himself gives a nostalgic account of the great 1934 team. Those curious to learn how Wild Bill overpowered a turkey with his cornet, how Dizzy Gillespie wrote *Swedish Suite* ('Bah! Bah! Boppity bah! Snow! Snow! Snow! Very, very, *very* cold!'), or what Fats Waller actually says on his banned records will find these and other matters fully dealt with. And finally there is Eddie Condon himself. At 51, this dapper alcoholic chum of Bix, with his nominal guitar-work and failed wisecracks, runs his own night-club, writes a column, and is qualifying as 'a legend'. If this personality gets in one's light occasionally, one has to remember that for thirty years it has been synonymous with a particularly honest and vital kind of music that for some has been the most consistently enjoyable thing in jazz, and a good deal of this spirit informs the book. This is only one reason why it is worth buying.

Mr Horricks's study of the Basie band from its inception was no doubt published to catch the interest aroused by the Count's recent visit, but for every reader won by the 1957 group there will be ten more who are thinking of the Decca recordings of 1937–9. Both, however, will be well satisfied. Mr Horricks deals at length not only with Basie and Kansas City but with all his sidemen through the years, and there are eight pages of photographs and a discography by Alun Morgan for good measure. It is a rather wordy book (getting off to a terrible start by quoting Henry Miller to the effect that Basie is a descendant of Rimbaud), and only suggests what a really first-hand biography of a coloured band would be like, but it is full of information and should not be missed by any student of what I have heard misleadingly described as the black art.[8]

Truth, 26 July 1957

3
Jazz

THE STORY OF JAZZ by Marshall Stearns (Sidgwick & Jackson, 30s)

Marshall Stearns Sc.B. (Yale) and Ph.D. (Harvard) approaches jazz not only with his own considerable resources (he is Director of the Institute of Jazz Studies[9]) but those of social history, musicology, economics and bibliography to produce this scholarly treatise. He unravels where jazz came from (150 pages of this), and where it seems to be going: there is, admittedly, some aboriginal anecdotage, including a pitiful psychiatrist's report on Buddy Bolden I haven't seen before; but there is also, for instance, a contention that bop is no more than a stage in harmonic evolution such as classical music underwent after Debussy and Wagner.[10]

In short, it's an intellectual's guide to jazz, and unlikely to be bettered for many years. Dr Stearns clings to the party line (white men good, black men better) and treats all branches of the music (including Chano Pozo) as equally significant.[11] But this does not spoil his book, whose only faults are the omission of English catalogue numbers, getting the date of *Sons and Lovers* wrong, and not mentioning Pee Wee Russell in all its 367 pages.

Truth, 6 December 1957

4
Harsh and Bitter-Sweet

KING JOE OLIVER by Walter C. Allen and Brian A. L. Rust (Sidgwick & Jackson, 224 pp., 1s)

LADY SINGS THE BLUES by Billie Holiday (Barrie Press, 228pp., 16s)

The lives of early jazzmen were often peculiarly hard. Unable to see their art outside a world where harsh exploitation was the rule, they were also at the mercy of the American economic climate and the fashions of show business. When their strength and originality left them, too often they returned to a miserable and obscure poverty, with nothing remaining of their work but a few recordings on a soon-defunct label. Very few are lucky enough twenty years after their death to receive the care and devotion that Messrs Allen and Rust have given to the life and works of the Negro cornet-player Joseph 'King' Oliver. There is something almost Henchardian[12] about the story they so painstakingly tell. Born in New Orleans in 1885, Oliver was one of that city's leading jazzmen by 1912: the closing of the red-light district sent him north to Chicago in 1917, where by 1923 his success had reached its height, with his first recordings, but from this time on luck turned against him. He stayed too long in Chicago: his pupil, Louis Armstrong, got to New York first, and when Oliver arrived in 1927 all the best jobs but one were taken, and this (at the new Cotton Club) Oliver mulishly refused because the salary was too low. It went instead to the young Ellington.[13] Then came the depression, and after this Oliver began to lose his teeth: for several years he toured the southern states with inferior musicians, struggling with bad pay and endless mishaps to the bands' kits and motor-bus, and by 1937 he was poor and ill and bandless in Savannah, working as a janitor in a pool-room. He died the following year, aged 53, just before the New Orleans revival got under way that might have brought him fame once more.

Allen and Rust rightly insist that Oliver was a great player with a great influence. Their work is a piece of scholarship: it does not have the warmth of that by Frederic Ramsey in 'Jazzmen,'[14] and they do not quote Oliver's moving letters to his sister ('I open the pool rooms at 9 a.m. and close at 12 midnite. If the money was only half as much as the hours I'd be all set . . . '), but they have gone to enormous trouble to establish all that can be known about Oliver and his recordings. The 120–page discography is exhaustive, and where the facts are not known all relevant opinion is tabled instead. It is a magnificent piece of research, which if it dealt with sphragistics or medieval price-fixing would surely win its authors a fellowship apiece.

Lady Sings The Blues is by contrast raw material. Published to coincide with the now-cancelled European visit of the coloured singer Billie Holiday (née Eleanora Fagan), it is an account in tough vernacular of Miss Holiday's life and hard times. The trouble with this kind of book is that natural artists can rarely say anything enlightening about their own art ('You just feel it, and when you sing it other people feel something too') or of the changes in artistic fashion ('Nowadays you have all this talk and bull and nothing's happening'), and the jazz interest is too often obscured by X-certificate stuff of doubtful necessity. But all Miss Holiday's admirers will want to read it, if only to see how her personality corresponds with her own special brand of bitter-sweet balladry (in spite of the title, she is not a blues-singer). When one reads that she once had to black her face in order to be as dark as the band she was fronting, and that she never got more than a recording fee for making all her finest recordings, one wonders, really, how the sweetness crept in.

Guardian, 13 June 1958

5
Bad Bold Beauty

'Henry James said of American cities, "So there it all is, arrange it as you can. Poor dear bad bold beauty, there must indeed be something about her . . . " The same can be said of American jazz.' Yes, it is the American jazz intellectual again, this time Dr Barry Ulanov, 40–year-old Assistant Professor at Columbia, editor of *Metronome*,[15] concert promoter, and jazz historian. By issuing two of his works in the same week his publishers provide an extended view of his approach, which is much freer from cultural excesses than the above quotation would suggest (unlike the English writer who can only get to Basie by way of Baudelaire): rather, his method is a somewhat solemn conflation of sources, none of them especially original, guided by the principle that jazz is an art form and must be thought of as such, and that social and anthropological and commercial considerations must be kept well in their place. In *A History of Jazz In America* (Hutchinson, 30s; first published in 1952, and not 1958 as the publishers assert) Dr Ulanov retells the familiar tale from 1900 onwards in New Orleans, Chicago, New York, and elsewhere, until it is 1950 and the music of Bolden and King Joe Oliver is in the keeping of such as John La Porta, who resembles 'a librarian in an institution devoted to research on dead Australian birds' and who gets his kicks from transcribing Bach. Dr Ulanov resists the temptation to be smart or tendentious, but his discreet withdrawals of sympathy from Bechet and Jelly Roll Morton prepare the reader for a quickening of the tempo after 1940 is reached, and for the revelation that Dr Ulanov not only likes the moderns but thinks they are an improvement on much that preceded them. Of New Orleans he writes: 'A beginning is a beginning [and] this was an unusually good beginning, but . . . what came after was often good, too—and sometimes better.' As a jazz historian, he is Wells rather than Gibbon.[16] The course of jazz in his view is a progressive acceptance and assimilation of new technical means of expression: the revivalist—Lu Watters, for instance—who will not leave 'the stagnating security to be found in playing in and around familiar chords' is bound to lose not only his audience but also his inspiration. The future lies with the jazz musician competent to explore poly– and atonality in his search for fresher and maturer ways of self-expression. Well, perhaps so.

A Handbook of Jazz (Hutchinson, 15s), guardedly introduced by Kingsley Amis,[17] is less certain of purpose. Dr Ulanov claims that he is trying to unite traditionalist and modern: his chapter-headings ('A Capsule History of Jazz,' 'The Instruments of Jazz,' 'The Schools of Jazz,' &c.) resemble those of a crammer's primer, but the articles themselves do not inter-relate and have the air of a round-up of periodical pieces in factitious unity. There is a glossary of jazz terms (always a tedious item), a dictionary of jazz players (a brief check revealed the absence of, for a start, Bob Scobey, Art Hodes, Josh White, Blind Lemon Jefferson and Tab Smith) and one of those charts that show what has happened in jazz and the other arts since 1900 (nothing has happened in literature since 1949 except something called 'The Cypresses Believe In God'). Of rather more value is a specimen library of jazz LPs—a core collection of 37 records with another 74 to be added as taste and means direct. Here again readers may amuse themselves by spotting omissions: the biggest is King Oliver's records of 1923–4. The most interesting essay, 'The Place of Jazz,' tackles the paradox of how jazz, a form of art with so small a range of means and effects, can yet, as Dr Ulanov bluntly says, 'stir certain feelings which are apparently universal.' This is indeed the central jazz mystery, and Dr Ulanov's solution—that it is a music specifically evolved by urban civilisation, with both the attendant limitations and enormous potential audience—seems reasonable enough.

The Decca Book of Jazz, edited by Peter Gammond (Muller, 40s), reminds me of a little book by Leonard Hibbs published in 1937 called 'Twenty-One Years of Swing Music,' which presented a history of jazz in terms of the Brunswick-Decca-Vocalion catalogue, with sometimes curious results. The Decca group has now repeated this venture, and is big enough to do it properly, with only an occasional discographical lacuna to show the book's *raison d'être*. One cannot help wishing they had followed their 1937 example and given the job to one man. Twenty-five essays by as many writers, laced with photographs and with a 76–page discography, cannot add up to the comprehensive study of jazz it purports to be; really it is no more than 25 scampers, of varying thoroughness, through the same number of somewhat arbitrarily chosen fields. The result is a 400–page book with a constant air of condensation. As it is, Ernest Borneman and Francis Newton are good and thorough on the African element and the classic blues singers. Stanley Dance retells the Ellington story pleasantly, and there is a fascinating piece of local history from Tony Hall. Steve Race is wasted on the swing era (and nobody deals with Brubeck),[18] and some other contributions fall markedly below mediocrity. Burnett James rounds it all off by asking if jazz and classical music can't get together. I should say that happened about ten years ago. The problem now is to get them apart.

Guardian, 29 August 1958

6
Such Sweet Thunder

DUKE ELLINGTON: HIS LIFE AND MUSIC edited by Peter Gammond (Phoenix House, 25s)

SECOND CHORUS by Humphrey Lyttelton (MacGibbon & Kee, 15s)

On Sunday, October 5, for the first time since George V was on the throne and Ramsay MacDonald at Downing Street, London will hear Duke Ellington and his orchestra. For 30 years this remarkable man has coaxed from successive teams of musicians that unique blend of composition and improvisation, flamboyance and restraint, programme music and down-to-earth jazz utterance for which his name is famous; this symposium, an occasional celebration rather than a critical assessment, mixes historical exposition, candid reporting, and selective discography with equal adroitness. The book gets a magnificent start from Richard O. Boyer's extended *New Yorker* study (and, stylistically, never recovers), which is supported by Daniel Halperin's reminiscences of Ellington musicians over the years. These pieces tether the music firmly to the hard and ordinary life the Duke and his men lead. A well-documented account of his recording career is followed by notes on soloists, with representative records, and a final skeleton discography on the useful basis of what is available. Further essays deal with Ellington as pianist and composer: by the end the reader knows how he resembles Delius as well as how Ray Nance eats his soup. I am sorry that no one saw fit to tell the story of Ellington's reaction to Shakespeare, whom he read before writing 'Such Sweet Thunder': 'You know what? All these lines have five beats.'[19]

Very properly, the book insists on the pictorial or even literary origin of Ellington's music: 'In my writing there's always a mental picture ... in the old days, when a guy made a lick, he'd say what it reminded him of ... That's the way I was raised up in music.' Or, as Burnett James says, 'His basic aim is to portray in sound the life of the American Negro population.' Someone might have added that, as in most pictorial music, the programme note seems irrelevant whenever the piece is successful, like scaffolding dismantled after use. The comparison of Ellington and Jelly Roll Morton is made but never pursued: how different in spirit are 'Black and Tan Fantasy' and 'Deep Creek.' And the recordings: how much did they owe to studio balance (witness the let-down of the rhythm-section here in 1933)? Why have Ellington's soloists (with about three exceptions) been so much less compelling outside his band? Why are 'Jack The Bear,' 'In a Jam,' and 'Echoes of the Jungle' not currently available? Perhaps the gramophone companies will yet do the honours in their own way. But no doubt it will all seem beside the point on October 5.

In Humphrey Lyttelton Britain has that rare thing, an articulate jazz man. His latest autobiographical instalment might have been provoked by the questions one would ask if given the opportunity: Why have you changed your line-up? Do you think Armstrong is finished? Did Condon's tour deserve to flop? Isn't tape surgery making nonsense of recorded jazz? And Humph provides the answers: if his manner is breezy, banal and dictaphonic, it is also level-headed and fairly good-natured, and *he knows what he is talking about.* For the addicts, the text is garnished with drawings, photographs, and a discography up to March, 1958.

Guardian, 30 September 1958

7
Mouldie Figges[20]

THE HEART OF JAZZ by William L. Grossman and Jack W. Farrell (Vision, 42s)

The interest of this book lies in its unashamed partiality. Every schoolboy knows that around 1940 a new generation of coloured musicians, bored to death with traditional harmonies and rhythms, began to devise a 'cool' antithesis to hot jazz that has since been enthusiastically taken up by young white and coloured players alike. This music bore the same degree of resemblance to the jazz of Bolden and Bix as 'The Waste Land' did to 'Idylls of the King,' and there was much pleasure to be had from the sight of suddenly antiquated traditionalists trying to swallow this new sound smilingly and see it as a natural development of the familiar tracks of their faithful old 78s.

Americans Grossman and Farrell will have none of this. If Barry Ulanov is the Leavis of modernism, they are, say, the Sir John Squire.[21] Students of literature will recognise the tone of such sentences as 'The quest for novelty in "modern" jazz is by no means confined to discursion into the exotic. It is part of the "modern" jazz-man's day-to-day, feverish, brain-tormenting burden,' and phrases such as 'utterly un-Christian content' and 'emotional gibberish' reinforce the impression of another Old Guard dying but not surrendering. 'The music is clever and interesting, but where is the deep appeal to the God-loving soul of man?'

A lot of people are going to deride this book and its authors' passionate adherence to the New Orleans tradition, to George Lewis and Bunk

Johnson and Kid Ory and the latter-day Frisco revivalists.[22] Admittedly Grossman and Farrell are so square they could play snooker with dice. But a generation immune to *Modernismus* in other arts may be more inclined to listen to their claim that the heart of jazz lies in the religious vitality of New Orleans music, even couched in the elephantine archaisms of Lu Watters and Turk Murphy. At any rate, their lively exposition of this style will send many back to the records of its exponents.

Guardian, 7 November 1958

8

Blues from the Brickyards

'Now, of course,' as the *New Yorker* recently pictured a Soviet music master telling his shaven-headed class, 'we're all familiar with the story of how jazz came up the Don from Rostov.' Not any more we're not. British-born Leonard Feather, who exported himself to America during the thirties, has cross-examined a number of old-timers such as W. C. Handy, Eubie Blake, and Willie 'The Lion' Smith, and in *The Book of Jazz* (Arthur Barker, 21s) he gives their astounding replies: 'I was playing it myself in Baltimore in 1898 and we called it ragtime ... '; 'The blues comes from the brickyards in Haverstraw, New York, where those coloured people worked in the brickyards ... '; 'When there were dozens of great musicians in the East, you couldn't find but two or three good piano players in the whole of New Orleans ... '; 'New Orleans just happened to get the publicity.' This dearest of legends, then—the multi-racial, Afro-European musical stew reaching its flashpoint in the 'carres' and 'bagnios' of the most exciting city in the world—this most persistent of traditions must, it seems, be abandoned. Jazz was born in New Orleans, Indianapolis and Baltimore; in Florida, Tennessee, and Alabama; in Texas and Oklahoma, Philadelphia, and New York—everywhere, in fact, where there were Negro communities with dances, funerals, and parades in need of musical accompaniment. That is, if we believe the old-timers.

There is nothing else as startling as this in the book, which is largely framed as a series of tepid historical accounts of the roles of different jazz instruments, which, though interesting, would have been better if punctuated with record numbers. Much more fun can be had out of *The New Yearbook of Jazz* (Arthur Barker, 35s), which is the second supplement to

Feather's *Encyclopaedia of Jazz*, containing a 50–page block of additional biographies. These have got around to Barber and Lyttelton and Yusef Lateef (real name William Evans), and bring the previous entries up to date from 1956 to 1958. Good support is given by a miscellany of articles and features, notably 'The Jazzman as Critic,' which gives the comments of jazz players on records played to them without previous identification. These are often unexpected: 'Do they expect to sell many of these?' (Eddie Condon); 'They could be Eskimos for all I know' (Roy Eldridge); 'It's one of those bop records in the sense that I detest it' (Sy Oliver); 'They should all be punched in the face' (Dinah Washington). They are even more amusing when you know what they are talking about. Well laced with action shots, mostly from TV shows.

Bix Beiderbecke, the incredible white cornetist who died in 1931, has been the unlucky subject of a good deal of 'glamour' journalism, and inspired the novel 'Young Man with a Horn,' by Dorothy Baker, all of which has served to inflate his memory into a jazz legend which has rarely graduated from sensationalism. Beiderbecke's ideal biographer might have been Scott Fitzgerald, who would have retained the romance of his career while recognising the tragedy of his character. Charles Wareing and George Garlick in *Bugles for Beiderbecke* (Sidgwick & Jackson, 25s) have set their faces against 'the Bix story.' They seem to have intended a sober assess-ment, but stylistically at least it has ended in sesquipedalian agony, due to their preference for 'posterior in date to' over 'later,' and a faint yet cumbersome facetiousness.

Nevertheless, this is a serious book and a great deal of trouble has gone into it. They incline to defend the Whiteman Orchestra, examine with great care how much influence Emmett Hardy could chronologically have had on their subject, and report (with what justification they do not say) that what Bix liked Bessie Smith to sing was not the blues but 'I'll See You in My Dreams.' They do not take up the question, which all previous literature on the subject has suggested to my mind, of how far Bix was mentally competent. References and an index would have given their contentions firmer grounding, both as regards the text and also the discography, which differs on several points of detail from that given in 'Jazz Directory.' It seems that Howdy Quicksell (banjo) not only did not arrive half-way through the recording of 'Davenport Blues,' he was not even on the session. No doubt there will be a come-back on this in the proper quarters at a posterior date.

Guardian, 20 March 1959

19

9
Jazz in Society

Editors' note: *The next two pieces have been run together, for though written as separate commissions, they centre on the same book. 'Francis Newton' is a pseudonym of Eric Hobsbawm, the Marxist historian made a Companion of Honour in 1998.*

THE JAZZ SCENE by Francis Newton (MacGibbon & Kee, 21s)

Most books on jazz—and there are a great many by now—come from America, for to add to its history or anecdote requires firsthand acquaintance with its sources and an authoritative way with the American language. It is a truism, however, that jazz had to come to Europe to be appreciated, and as its appeal spreads European writers should be increasingly able to make their own contribution—that long cultural or sociological view that the American is often too close to take.

This Mr Francis Newton is well fitted to do. A jazz critic who is also a professional historian, his knowledge and love of the music is continually touching off academic speculations in his mind, and in *The Jazz Scene* he has attempted to combine some of these with an orthodox introduction for the layman.

Personally I should have preferred the speculations neat. It is time publishers realised that there are no laymen in jazz nowadays, and although Mr Newton does the up-the-river-from-New-Orleans, who-played-what routine well, it is a waste of his time. However, when this duty is done, Mr Newton unleashes his ideas and investigations on a great variety of topics—popular music, the jazz business, the jazz audi-ence—and, although these come at the reader rather haphazardly, they seem grouped around two fundamental questions: how can the enormous popularity of jazz be accounted for, and what kind of interactions—social and economic—have taken place between the music and the society that produced it?

* * *

Mr Newton is really a jazz sociologist (he denies it on one page, but elsewhere asserts 'jazz in society is what this book is about'), and he is clearly fascinated by the sudden efflorescence of this minor folk art into the unique emotional language of our century. The answer he proposes is that many of us nowadays *are* slaves, emotionally or economically, and 'because Negroes are or were oppressed even among the poor and powerless, their cries of protest are more poignant and more over-whelming, their cries of hope more earth-shaking than other peoples', and have found, even in words, the most unanswerable expression ... It is not merely a voice of protest: it is a natural loudspeaker.'

Mr Newton's second theme is linked with the development of jazz, its continual retreat before its commercial promoters. Although, as he sen-sibly says, such professionalism is a jazz player's living and commercial recordings his only hold on posterity, the difficulty is that each sincerely felt innovation is immediately exploited into a cliché and has to be abandoned. 'The evolution of jazz has constantly snatched the victory of fine achievement out of the disasters of commercialisation, and today perhaps out of academic etiolation.' Thus the traditional revival was a flight from swing, and bop a flight from traditionalism; now bop is a worse cliché than traditional, and Mr Newton is not hopeful about the future: 'It is more than probable that whatever jazz is played in the future will be unpalatable to many critics on musical or social grounds.' There are times when reading Mr Newton's account of this essentially working-class art, the course of jazz seems almost a little social or economic parable, and certainly the social historian Mr Newton never misses a trick.

Every intelligent jazz-lover will want to read *The Jazz Scene* (and 'jazz enthusiasts as a group are distinctly above the national average in education'). Mr Newton has little charm as a writer, but what he has to say on subjects as diverse as the element of social protest in jazz and the price of LPs fully compensates for it. His book is, however, not all free-hand theorising. Mr Newton keeps coming back to his over-mastering passion, the blues—to Bessie Smith, 'a major tragic artist,' to Ma Rainey, Blind Lemon, Joe Turner, and the hosts of anonymous strollers through the Deep South who played their guitars with knife-blades and made unforgettable moan. His palpable love of their music convinces the reader of his sincerity, even if some of his contentions start rather than settle arguments.

Observer, 31 May 1959

10
Music of the Negro

One cannot consider jazz without being astonished at the speed with which it has gained ascendancy over popular musical taste in societies and cultures very different from that which produced it. Indeed, there is a curious logic in the world's enthusiastic response to the music of the Negro, as if in some gigantic Jungian case-history where salvation is shown to lie in whatever is most feared and despised. Why, when white folk-music is so patently defunct, should coloured folk-music prove so potent a substitute? As Mezz Mezzrow said, 'I had plenty to thank those coloured boys for. They not only taught me their fine music: they made me feel good.' What emotional release is at work here?

Mr Francis Newton, social historian and jazz critic of the *New Statesman*, is continually aware of questions like these, and in *The Jazz Scene* (MacGibbon & Kee, 21s), he makes repeated forays in the direction of answering them, meantime laying down a more conventional exposition of the history, character, and social background of jazz. At times Mr Newton seems a little at odds with himself: there can be no good reason why a British intellectual should be moved by Bessie Smith or Blind Lemon Jefferson, and yet he is: a sociology of jazz would be an absurd conception, and yet clearly such a phenomenon should be explicable by him in social terms. If our cult of jazz were another exotic minority fad, like Negro masks or flamenco dancing, it could be dismissed as an attempt to 'compensate for the moral deficiencies of [our] life,' but what about working-class teenagers who rock and skiffle as to the manner born?—or the middle-class clerk whom jazz introduces to the vast para-scholarship of discography and the technical expertise of hi-fi? Why should the Aldermaston marchers have followed a *jazz* band?

Mr Newton's answers should be sought in his own pages, and if they are not always convincing they are invariably stimulating: it is a pleasure to read a jazz writer who can speak seriously without becoming stilted or absurd and has a clear sight of the fact that 'no orthodox American composer is a genuinely international figure: all are provincial figures blown up by local pride.[23] But Louis Armstrong, Bessie, Charlie Parker are accepted without question all over the world.'

Jazz at any moment takes its character from what the young men are playing, and in *These Jazzmen of Our Time* (Gollancz, 18s) Mr Raymond Horricks presents a series of close-ups by divers hands of the players who are reshaping jazz to-day. Born mostly in the 1920s, these fifteen or so exponents include surviving pioneers of the modern movement (Thelonious Monk), leaders identified with the musical approach of their groups (Mulligan, Lewis), the arrangers Gil Evans and Gigi Gryce, and straightforward soloists such as J. J. Johnson, Miles Davis, and Sonny Rollins. All but three are Negroes, which clearly indicates how coloured musicians have succeeded in wresting back the initiative in deciding what jazz shall sound like, and a large proportion are composer-arrangers, demonstrating that jazz is no longer thought of exclusively in terms of improvisation. All of them, it need hardly be said, use the modern idiom.

The prevailing mood, therefore, is one of excited experiment ('Why don't you get a piano player? and what's that stuff he's playing?') and some attempt is made to convey the kind of innovation each player has made or is making. Most of the studies, however, inevitably fall somewhere between the profile, the potted biography, and the musicological analysis, and not all the writers are able to produce a unified impression for this reason. Benny Green on John Lewis and Mr Horricks on Milt Jackson, Brubeck and the two drummers Max Roach and Art Blakey are the most informative pieces for the uninitiated.

Guardian, 31 July 1959

11
A Racial Art

BLUES FELL THIS MORNING by Paul Oliver (Cassell, 30s)

When you sing the blues, you sing a rhymed couplet (with the first line repeated) against a twelve-bar progression of the common chord on the keynote, the chord of the sub-dominant, the chord of the dominant, and the chord of the dominant seventh. It is a loose, monotonous form, easily fitted to physical movement like lifting or scrubbing, and it is the American Negro's most characteristic expression. Into it have gone his loves, his hates, his protests, his whole emotional life: you will find no dream-boats or June moons, but more likely:

> Lord, I really don't think no man's love can last
> Lord, I really don't think no man's love can last
> They love you to death then treat you like a thing of the past.

Blues singers—the strolling man with a guitar, or the vaudeville *artiste* in bangles and silk dress—became conservers and originators of a racial art. Since 1920, literally thousands of their records have been made for the American Negro market, their harsh voices shouting against out-of-condition studio pianos or some portable accompaniment such as guitar or harmonica, but very few of these have found their way over here. Leroy Carr, Peetie Wheatstraw, Blind Boy Fuller, Arthur Crudup, Bumble Bee Slim and a host of others are known to Britain only by a few tracks courageously put out by minority jazz labels. I would willingly sacrifice the next few stacks of 'Ella Sings Ivor Novello,' or whatever it will be,[24] for

Arthur Crudup's 'No More Lovers,' and rejoice that there are signs that interest in the vocal blues is growing.

* * *

One such is the work of Mr Paul Oliver. His long researches in the blues have changed his original intention to write one book about them into an intention to write two, of which *Blues Fell This Morning* is the first. In it, using the transcribed lyrics from 350 records, he describes the Negro's way of life as revealed in his blues. His method is to take a particular area of experience, quote from lyrics which portray or comment on it, and add his own clarification or embellishment. This latter is often startling. On the couplet, for example:

> Yes, I'm sinking, sinking down below my grave, (*twice*)
> Done had a good time, but, Lord, how I done paid

Mr Oliver can make the grim gloss that among the first 100,000 Negroes drafted there was an average 241.2 syphilitics in every 1,000 (the comparable white figure was 18.5); when a man sings, 'Say, I'm goin' to Detroit, I'm gonna get myself a job (*twice*), I'm tired of layin' around workin' on this starvation farm,' Mr Oliver can tell us all about share-cropping on the one hand, and Mr Ford and the tar-paper 'shack-towns' in industrial cities during the Depression on the other.

It is a drab and depressing recital. On the evidence of the blues alone the Negro's life is composed of poverty, extortion, lust, crime, superstition and death, together with a generalised *Angst* (having the blues) that the contemplation of these induces. Mr Oliver seems ready to imply that, by and large, this must be accepted: one looks in vain for acknowledgement of the separate corpus of Gospel singing except as a failure to 'meet the present world on its own terms,' as the blues does. If the Negro appears in his songs to be crude, defeatist and unspiritual, that is because his conditions have made him so, and he should be praised for his realism. Too often, however, Mr Oliver deserts social comment and falls into what is no more than a mournful paraphrase of his material in the accents of a silent-film caption:

> Her arms still feel the warmth of her husband's love, and his fond words even
> as he betrayed her love still remain in her mind, their sweetness now turned
> bitter as gall.

His kind of exegesis teaches his readers the difference between a buffet flat and a barrelhouse flat, but not Bogardus's race-relations cycle.[25] It is perhaps inevitable, also, that no one could deduce from Mr Oliver's transcriptions the vital joyous subtlety of his originals.[26] This is a pity, for it is precisely this achieved paradox of turning suffering, misery and injustice into a new kind of music that has delighted half the world that is the American Negro's unique contribution to our century.

Observer, 27 March 1960

12
A Real Musicianer

Sidney Bechet died in Paris last May on his sixty-second birthday. His life had been different from the other great New Orleans jazzmen. He had not become a national institution, like Armstrong, an embittered survivor, like Morton, or a melodramatic rediscovery, like Johnson. Thickset, independent, undemonstrative, yet capable to the end of his days of fits of temperament, Bechet remained essentially a jobbing clarinet and soprano-saxophone player, happiest with small groups where his big tone and autocratic personality could be dominant. By nature he was a traveller: he played before King George V in 1919 (in Buckingham Palace, by his own account), in Moscow in 1925, and in Berlin at the Haus Vaterland in 1931 (there are photographs to prove this fantastic foray into the Isherwood country). Altogether it is not surprising that he should have ended up in Paris with that Henry Miller of jazz, Mezz Mezzrow, nor that the French jazz world should thereupon have deified him. For fifteen post-war years Bechet ruled traditional French jazz through the bands of Luter and Reweliotty—and most of all, of course, by his own excellent example.

For once one feels the French were right. Bechet's tone was not to everyone's taste; he had some appalling clichés; but the force and sweep of his solos were unequalled in lyric dignity. There are not many perfect things in jazz, but Bechet playing the blues could be one of them. This being so, it is regrettable that *Treat It Gentle* (Cassell, 25s) falls so short of an official biography. A Miss Joan Williams persuaded Bechet to tape-record his recollections, which reached 1936 by this means: Mr Desmond Flower, coming to transcribe this material, got Bechet to take up the tale again, but the musician's death occurred before the final chapters could be more than sketched in. The medium encourages repetitive pontification, and too often Bechet tries to tell us about jazz ('that love-feeling has to find the music-feeling' & c.), when what we want to hear about is Bechet, but even so there is plenty of interest. Bechet gives characteristic accounts of Panassié's 1938 sessions[27] and the Bunk Johnson *furore*, and unintentionally amuses by grumbling that Louis Armstrong didn't play what they'd agreed he should in '2.19 Blues' and the others ('he's got himself a name and he's got to perform up to that name'). Believers in collective improvisation please note. But on the other hand he is warmly generous about Bessie Smith (with whom he toured in 1922), Duke Ellington ('he's a real musicianer'), and Eddie Condon ('there's no one done more than Eddie'). 'The music' was everything to Bechet: 'Me, I want to explain myself so bad. I want to have myself understood. And the music, it can do that. The music, it's my whole story.' Many remarkable photographs are included, and a catalogue of recordings lacking personnels, places of recording and English recording numbers.

I can't imagine anyone paying 30s for *This Is Jazz* (Newnes) and yet in some ways it is the most satisfying kind of jazz book. As its editor Ken Williamson points out, too serious an approach can miss the point of jazz altogether, and an agreeably light touch characterises these twenty-odd essays and bunches of action photographs (jazz photographs have a particular joyous excitement all their own). The American, Whitney Balliett, is incomparably the best writer, and another American, Kenneth Hulsizer, contributes the most interesting article, an account of the latter-day Jelly Roll Morton in Washington ('he had never heard of a record collector'). Other good stuff is purveyed by Iain Lang, Francis Newton, Barry Ulanov, and Stanley Dance. Humphrey Lyttelton, in a mildly satiric survey of the local jazz situation, wonders why intellectuals favour traditional. Maybe because it's the best kind, which they know, being intellectuals.

Guardian, 8 April 1960

13
The Critic as Hipster

There is a kind of imaginative journalism that one suspects has its roots in Wilde's 'The Critic as Artist.' When Cardus[28] writes 'During his first few overs, Grace's bat was like a stout door bolted against evil,' or Liebling[29] reports a boxer throwing a right 'like an old woman throwing a pie,' Wilde's sentence about the relation of the critic to the work of art being precisely that of the artist to the visible world comes irresistibly to mind. Whitney Balliett, jazz critic of the *New Yorker*, is the latest recruit in this field. 'Russell can be devastating in a slow blues. Sidling softly into the lower register, where he gets a tone that is a cross between the low thyroid murmurings of Joe Marsala and the bejowled utterances of Jimmie Noone, he will issue, after some preliminary blinking and squinting (as if he had just entered a bright room from a dark street), a series of crablike, irregularly staccato phrases, each shaken by a bone-worrying vibrato and each clamped tightly against its predecessor, lest any distractions leak in to cool off what he has in mind. After this, he may rocket up a couple of octaves and adopt a quavering, gnashing manner, or he may introduce dark, stuttering growls which seem to lacerate what he is playing ... ' Now this sort of thing can easily become precious, and in some quarters Balliett is dismissed as a fancypants. Yet it is difficult not to enjoy the sensibility that notes that although in slow tempos Ben Webster's tone is 'soft and enormous,' in middle tempos 'it shrinks ... as if it were too bulky to carry at such a pace.' Nor is it always pressed into the service of reverence. An 'amorphous group,' featuring two vibraphones, a trombone, Max Roach and Dinah Washington, 'went on forever, particularly in a vibraphone duet, which after a time achieved an effect like coconuts raining on a tin roof.'

The Sound of Surprise (William Kimber, 25s) is a collection of pieces written for the *New Yorker* during the fifties, and it is safe to say that anyone who has formed a taste for Balliett there will want them on his shelves. Many of them are record reviews (the remainder are descriptions of concerts) but escape the usual limitations of this form by reason of the author's willingness to range around his set subject and use his personal experience to vivify his references ('Red Allen, the tireless *sad-faced* trumpeter'). They provide a good wide-angled view of jazz in the States over the period immediately following the establishment of the music of Parker, Monk and Gillespie, and bring home to the British reader how extraordinarily many kinds of this music can exist simultaneously. Though Balliett's sympathies lie to the cool of mainstream, he is equally eloquent on Jelly Roll Morton, Bechet and Sidney Catlett, and indeed there is hardly a cross word in the book: one suspects that his dislikes can only be what he fails to mention.[30] Those with jazz-loving friends have one Christmas-present problem the less.

Jazz, edited by Nat Hentoff and Albert McCarthy (Cassell, 25s), is a group of twelve specialist essays arranged to make a rough history of the music. By comparison with Balliett they are on the stodgy side, while some of the topics—New Orleans, the blues, boogie-woogie, and so on—are something less than fresh, but Franklin S. Driggs covers the relatively unfamiliar field of the bands of Kansas City and the South-west readably and at length. Nat Hentoff rounds the collection off with a too-short grumble about the extent to which jazz is dependent on the booker and the promoter, and the ways it is tricked and debased in consequence. (Nor is this confined to America. Ken Colyer recently reported in the 'Melody Maker' the result of putting his own checker on the door to count the attendance.) There are interesting descriptions of Ellington's earliest records by Gunther Schuller.

Jazz Street, a photographic exploration of the world of jazz by Dennis Stock (André Deutsch, 55s), presents a wide range of pictures, some retaining kinship with the old band groups of tuxedos and harvest-festival of instruments, others toppling over into the self-importance and hysteria of theatrical portraiture. Beside the historical richness of Keepnews and Grauer's 'Pictorial History of Jazz'[31] it seems thin and unmoving, yet the photography is often more skilful and the production considerably better. Many plates are action-shots, of necessity heavily chiaroscuro'd, and invest currently successful jazz artists with a kind of pompous informality. There is an uncomfortably sad one of Lester Young ('No, no one has come up and said Thank you'), and a splendid underlining of Mr Condon's growing resemblance to Miss Ivy Compton-Burnett. At first I was annoyed by a facetious portrayal of Pee Wee Russell, standing while his dog relieves itself on the pavement, but now I am inclined to think it the key picture in the collection.

Guardian, 25 November 1960

14
With Not-So-Silent Friends

Books about jazz fall into several groups. There are the 'as-told-to' autobiographies ('Buddy Bolden sure loved my Mama's red beans and rice'), the purely discographical (and when is the Gulbenkian Foundation going to enable Albert McCarthy to finish his monumental 'Jazz Directory', now stuck at Fred Longshaw?), the amorphous anthologies of articles and photos, the Pete-Lala's-to-Birdland[32] histories. What we have not had so far is the occasional personality-essayist, the Cardus or Newman of jazz, who will deploy themes of his own choosing with sufficient erudition and elegance to be both significant and pleasing. Whitney Balliett of the *New Yorker* might do it, and his 'Sound of Surprise' (1960) has both these necessary qualities, but being a collection of record and concert reviews does not qualify on formal grounds.

Mr Burnett James's *Essays on Jazz* (Sidgwick and Jackson, 16s), however, is so much the sort of thing I mean that I wish I could say it is entirely so. Unfortunately it isn't. Mr James is a shocking writer. He is facetious ('On Swinging Bach' begins: 'I do not, of course, refer to submitting [he means subjecting] Johann Sebastian Bach to capital punishment'). He is intolerably long-winded ('I do not advocate ... Still less do I contend ... Let us put this in a different way ... '). His mind wanders all over the place: an essay on Bix goes from Wordsworth and T. S. Eliot to Lang and Reinhardt, Teagarden and Harrison, Nichols and Goodman, occasionally cannoning off its ostensible subject as if by accident. He cannot resist dragging in culture-references ('Lester Young's mind possessed an almost Hazlitt-like sharpness'), and these are not always of the happiest ('Every reader knows that Wordsworth only stood revealed as one of the half-dozen or so greatest poets ever born of woman when he forgot his clever notions'). The not-infrequent misprints (Mendellsohn, Gillispie, Grappelley) add to an overall impression of immaturity.

This is a pity, for Mr James has a real feeling for jazz. He is acute, for instance, about Billie Holiday: ' . . . the determining factor for Ella or Sarah is what they get out of a song; with Billie it was what she put into it . . . A bad record by Ella or Sarah can be accepted at its face value . . . But a bad record by Billie caused a sudden stab of pain'; he does justice, as welcome as it is rare, to Bud Freeman as a 'dry' alternative to Coleman Hawkins long before Lester Young. There is an interesting essay on Oliver, rather typically entitled 'King Oliver as a Father-figure', in which he is seen as the stylistic progenitor not only of Armstrong but of Beiderbecke and (to my mind less questionably) Bubber Miley. (A History of Growling would be a nice essay-subject.) And in more general vein, Mr James's analogies between jazz and the great classical tradition of improvisation, and jazz and the music of the seventeenth century may at least provoke further discussion. Bach *does* go to town: one remembers Panassié's friend asking 'Is that Bach?' as the critic was picking out a Teschemacher[33] solo one-fingeredly on the piano.

As an authority on music, Mr James might be expected to have had more to say about the more musically adventurous moderns; for a jazz lover, he makes remarkably little mention of the blues. Very likely for all its good intentions his book will fall between these two classes of reader. This is much to be regretted, for we are now at a stage where the mass enthusiasm necessary to make jazz commercially viable needs educating in order to raise the standard of music it demands, and this kind of book would be admirably fitted to do it.

Guardian, 15 September 1961

15
Lives of the Poets

Reading the lives of jazzmen, one is struck by certain recurrent features. There is the instant and early recognition—often almost in infancy—of the music that is to be their destiny ('I kept asking the trumpet questions—how do you get all that stuff on the first valve?'). There is the dedicated practising on a schemed-for instrument. There is the resolute refusal to compromise with commercialism and the persistence in playing the 'right' kind of music in the teeth of public indifference or family hostility. And for some, there is unhappily the poverty and decay caused through drunkenness, ill-health, or simply some changed whim of the entertainment world. In a way it has been the jazzman who in this century has led 'the life of the Artist'. At a time when the established arts are generally accepted and subsidised with unenthusiastic reverence, he has had to suffer from prejudice or neglect in order to get the unique emotional language of our age recognised. And he has been enabled to do this by the intensity of his devotion to it. It is hard to think of the career of, say, Bix Beiderbecke or Charlie Parker without sensing that something of the emotion behind Wordsworth's

> We poets in our youth began in gladness,
> But thereof come in the end despondency and madness

is not entirely inappropriate in this context.

If despondency and madness do not figure in the life of *Django Reinhardt* by the celebrated French discographer Charles Delaunay (Cassell, 25s), there is none the less sufficient *dérèglement* to satisfy the most romantic. Django, who to the younger generation is probably no more than the

35

ame of a number by the MJQ,[34] was a gipsy: illiterate, fond of gambling, too proud to carry his own guitar, and almost entirely unreliable. He seems to have picked up jazz from local café and club bands, and drifted into fame in Paris while living in a caravan outside. Even during the period of his greatest success with Stephane Grappelli and the Quintet du Hot Club de France, he was always liable to disappear, fishing or simply following the nomadic instincts of his race, and he seems to have made little attempt to capitalise on his fame beyond demanding enormous fees. When, after the war, his dream of America was at last realised (he did not even take his guitar, imagining the guitar makers would compete for the privilege of giving him one), he had only a moderate success and was not sorry to return to France.

His death, from a stroke, at the age of 43 seems an inconclusive comma in a life running for the most part parallel to jazz rather than as part of its lifeline. The coming of modern jazz, though it led some people to lose interest in his astonishingly nimble and richly chorded improvisations, does not seem to have disconcerted him unduly: in the last year of his life he jammed with Dizzy Gillespie without embarrassment. The author provides a magnificent discography, taking up half the book, as if in acknowledgement that his text does not fully explain this extraordinary man.

Guardian, 24 November 1961

16
Bunk's Boy

George Lewis, the mild-mannered veteran New Orleans clarinettist, was 42 before the magazine *Look* brought him fame with a feature article. In consequence in the later forties his band was brought to New York to support that walking legend of New Orleans revivalism Bunk Johnson, and after Bunk's death continued in its own right: taking its particularly boisterous brand of jazz all over the States and to Britain and the Continent also. All this and more is told with almost motherly affection by the band's manager, Dorothy Tait, who under the name of Joy Allison Stuart wrote *Call Him George* (Peter Davies, 25s). In her presentation Lewis emerges as a modest, dignified man, of strong family feeling and devotion to his associates, who has led the hard life of the Negro musician without complaint: we learn, for instance, that, as so often, Lewis has never had a cent for the bulk of his records except the fee for making them. If the author is at times over-indulgent to her happily still-living subject, most readers will forgive her on account of his remarkable music which—even more remarkably—has won the praise of both Acker Bilk and Ornette Coleman.

Guardian, 1 December 1961

17
The Story of the Original Dixieland Jazz Band

by H. O. Brunn (Sidgwick & Jackson, 21s)

The first jazz record, if you have ever wondered, was made by a group of five white ad-libbers from New Orleans led by cornetist Nick LaRocca. It was released on March 7, 1917, by the Victor Talking Machine Company, while the Original Dixieland Jazz Band, as they called themselves, was currently astounding society patrons in the 400 Room at Reisenweber's, New York. Such was its success that next year Columbia sent a scout to find some rival combination. After three weeks he wired back 'NO JAZZ BANDS IN NEW ORLEANS'.

This book, first published in 1960 by the Louisiana State University Press and based largely on the LaRocca papers in the archives of New Orleans jazz at Tulane University, exemplifies the anecdote in two ways. In the first place it tells the story of this fabulous unit that so caught the imagination of war-time New York and post-war London, playing everywhere from the Savoy Hotel and King George V at the Victory Ball to the New York Zoo for a female hippopotamus named Miss Murphy (who promptly submerged). In the second, it is concerned to show, partly by implication but partly directly, that LaRocca's was indeed the 'original' jazz band, and therefore responsible for 'creating' jazz.

The band's history falls into two parts: 1916 to 1925, when LaRocca suffered a nervous breakdown, and from 1936 to 1938, an antiquarian revival to catch the germinating taste for Dixieland jazz which ended with a quarrel over money. The first was overwhelmingly the more important.

Those Victor records carried their fierce, formal syncopation far and wide, stimulating an entire white hot school (see, or rather hear, for instance, 'Dixieland Bands', Parlophone PMC 1171) that softened only with the escapist commercialism of the Depression. By the time the veterans (LaRocca was born in 1889) reunited, their music had been absorbed and developed to a point where its original form was hardly more than a curiosity.

Mr Brunn's thesis that the ODJB 'invented' jazz out of a kind of instrumental ragtime is put forward mainly by the staggering trick of completely omitting all reference to contemporary Negro New Orleans performers such as Bolden, Oliver, Bunk Johnson or Keppard. No reader of his book would suspect that the Negroes had anything to do with jazz at all. Can this be the official Southern view?[35] Undeniably the ODJB's recordings set the earliest national jazz pattern, but their success was more a commercial accident than proof of artistic pre-eminence—Victor, after all, had approached Keppard's Original Creole Band in 1916 (Keppard's reply was 'Nothin' doin', boys. We won't put our stuff on records for everybody to steal'). This utter lack of context is damaging. As for Columbia's talent-scout, someone should have told him that since Storyville closed the previous October, New Orleans was a bad bet. He should have gone to Chicago.

Listener, LXVII, 31 May, 1962

18
Should Jazz Be an Art?

*THE RELUCTANT ART: FIVE STUDIES IN THE GROWTH OF JAZZ by
Benny Green (MacGibbon & Kee, 21s)*

Let harmonies be oranges, says Mr Green, and the development of jazz is
like a juggling act which, having started with an isolated orange tossed
from hand to hand, today has the air thick with them, not all under
control. Its development has been, in short, a progressive musical complication, not very advanced when compared with that of music in general,
perhaps, but astonishingly rapid none the less, and to be understood only
by the musically educated.

To plot it, Mr Green discusses five key figures who have, so to speak,
added a few oranges to the act, though in choosing them he has taken their
general artistic and professional significance into account as well. Thus he
sees the life of Bix Beiderbecke (quite correctly in my view) not as a
meaningless decadence but as a search for increasing musical sophistication. Benny Goodman sought to ride out the Depression by perfecting his
technique, and was rewarded by becoming the first national brand-image
King of Swing. Lester Young, while responsible for no great harmonic
innovation, *sounded* so different that a whole 'alternative order' was
suddenly felt to be possible, and of course with Charlie Parker such an
order sprang into being. Only Billie Holiday, of Mr Green's selections,
seems lacking in this kind of significance, though no one would quarrel
with her inclusion in any jazz pantheon.

* * *

Mr Green himself is a trained musician and jazzman (he gets in a few shrewd side-swipes at critics who are not: the second-childhooders, the discographical train-spotters, the sociological culture-men), and his book is most valuable when he focuses the reader's attention on specific recorded examples of the nuances that make up these personal contributions to jazz. On these occasions his enthusiasm can be understood and shared. On others a certain shrillness mars his ability to persuade: his treatment of Goodman is unfairly jibing, and surely in 1962 there is no need to spend three pages hacking at 'Young Man With A Horn'. Nor is a sarcastic reference to Whitney Balliett of the *New Yorker* supported by the quality of Mr Green's own writing, which is spotted with the 'her range had shrunk to unmanageable proportions' kind of solecism.

The climax of the book is, fittingly, the last chapter on Parker, and Mr Green sets out clearly and even movingly the historical necessity of his breakthrough into chromaticism. Not only were the diatonic harmonies cramping: everything that could be done with them had been done already by the masters of the twenties and thirties. The young men had to find something new, or give up jazz altogether. Those listeners who cannot make the jump in appreciation from Young to Parker are denounced by Mr Green, not without a touch of triumphant arrogance, as 'dilettante followers for whom an affectation of jazz enthusiasm was a social asset or a personal vanity. After Parker you had to be something of a musician to follow the best jazz of the period.'

Clearly one could say a good deal on this point,[36] but assuming Mr Green is right it is hard to share his enthusiasm. What was so exciting about jazz was the way its unique, simple gaiety instantly communicated itself to such widely differing kinds of human being—Negro porters, Japanese doctors, King George VI. As a private language of musicians it will not be nearly so important. Reluctantly or not, it will have declined into an art.[37]

Observer, 23 September 1962

19

Jazz and the White Americans

JAZZ AND THE WHITE AMERICANS: THE ACCEPTANCE OF A NEW ART FORM by Neil Leonard (University of Chicago Press, $4.50)

It is ironical that the first American music to catch world attention should have originated among that nation's most despised section—the Negroes, who well within living memory had been regarded as a species of farm animal ('nobody killed, just a mule and a couple of niggers').[38] It must have been galling for Europe-orientated concert-goers of Boston and Philadelphia when Dvořák proclaimed that 'in the Negro melodies of America I discover all that is needed for a great and noble school of music';[39] when Ravel insisted on going to The Nest in Chicago to hear Jimmy Noone; when Milhaud and Honegger used jazz rhythms as if they took them seriously. For this jazz was not only a hideous cacophony played on old tins and saxophones, it was the very language of the brothels and speakeasies where it was played, and constituted a direct incitement to immorality, so menacing the entire fabric of society.

Dr Leonard, of the University of Pennsylvania, has set himself the fascinating task of tracing the stages by which white America, the America of the pulpits, editorials and school boards, came to accept the Negro's music. He describes how the initial rejection of it was twofold—aesthetic ('droning jerky incoherence') and moral ('Does Jazz Put The Sin In Syncopation?'), and how essentially the same device of refinement was used to overcome both, producing on the one hand the emasculated white dance music of the twenties, and on the other its June-moon lyrics with their studied avoidance of unpleasant elements. Dr Leonard prints charts showing how the rougher realisms retreated before such concepts as Personification of Nature, Dreams as a Solution to Unhappiness, and Intercourse treated with Abstract Periphrasis. Thus rendered acceptable to white ears, the new music was spread by the means of radio and phonograph, and appears to have provided a rare inversion of a musical Gresham's Law[40], for as listeners grew accustomed to it, popularity of the real undiluted article increased also.[41] By the middle of the thirties it was possible for a genuine jazz player such as Benny Goodman to command white popularity without soft-pedalling his jazz approach. Louis Armstrong appeared in a film. Duke Ellington played Carnegie Hall. Jazz became a school and university subject. 'By the early forties,' the narrative concludes, 'public complaints about jazz had virtually disappeared.'

Dr Leonard has drawn upon a wide variety of sources (his bibliography lists nearly 200 books and even more magazine and newspaper articles) to put together an important summary of historical material whose value is increased by the fugitive nature of the originals. Perhaps inevitably, however, the interest of his book does not quite match that of his subject. One reason for this is undoubtedly a certain negative vagueness that hangs about the word 'acceptance'; Dr Leonard spends too much time on the 'public complaint' aspect and not enough in analysing more positive manifestations. Although his references include publications dated as recently as 1960, too, his thesis hardly progresses beyond America's entry into the war; the acceptance of jazz, however, continued to progress, as shown, for instance, by the State Department-sponsored tours of Africa and the Middle East by Armstrong and Gillespie, or the Paul Winter concert in the White House. One wonders too how far America has stopped thinking of jazz as 'immoral': it is still fairly closely linked in the public mind with drug addiction, and it still largely depends for its existence on areas of business controlled by racketeers. The American Federation of Musicians is reputed never to have taken legal action on behalf of a jazz musician.

Much could be written, too, on the way that the early curiosity of classical composers has on the whole slackened, to be replaced by interest in the reverse direction by the younger musically-educated players who see jazz as at least in part a composer's music. There seems to be an agreement that academic music has far more to offer jazz than the other way round, in fact the fundamental rhythmic and tonal qualities of jazz seem to have proved unassimilable.[42] Lastly, one would expect a semi-sociological study of this kind to point out that the acceptance of jazz was to some degree bound up with the acceptance of the American Negro, and to try to trace this by some simple criterion such as the public permissibility of the mixed group. Considerations of this kind raise the question of whether jazz has ever accepted white America.[43] But that would be the beginning of another, different book.

Tempo, 64 (Spring, 1963)[44]

BIRD: THE LEGEND OF CHARLIE PARKER by Robert H. Reisner (MacGibbon & Kee, 30s)

When Charlie Parker died in March, 1955, he was 34, but the doctor judged him to be in his early sixties. An earlier psychiatric report called him 'a hostile, evasive personality with manifestations of primitive and sexual fantasies associated with hostility and gross evidence of paranoid thinking.' Baroness de Koenigswarter, in whose flat he died, said he was 'a relaxed type of person, and you sometimes hardly knew he was around.' This book's dust-jacket describes him as 'America's greatest artist.'

Clearly such statements require a lot of squaring to make a recognisable picture. Mr Reisner has gone to a great deal of trouble to collect 82 recollections of Parker from persons such as his mother, his second wife, managers Teddy Blume and himself, and jazzmen Miles Davis, Dizzy Gillespie, Earl Hines, Charlie Mingus, Buster Smith and many more. Unfortunately, having done so, he strings them together in a meaningless alphabetical order of recollector, as if purposely presenting a chaotically splintered image. Therefore we learn from Sadik Hakim (p. 103) that in 1942 people wouldn't play with Parker because he was too good long before Jay McShann remembers (p. 147) that in 1937 people wouldn't play with him because he was so bad.

What emerges is the son of a remarkable woman who was devoted to him ('He was my heart, you know') with an astounding natural musical gift, but whose ego suffered sharply from its first collision with the jazz world. They laughed at him ('I went home and cried and didn't play again for three months'). This seems to have led him to place a fantastic emphasis on professional musical technique: he could produce his poly-rhythmic chromatic sixteenths and thirty-seconds in any physical condition. His instinctive musical originality combined with his virtuosity to make him the leader of a group of young Negroes in the early forties who were pushing back the harmonic and rhythmic bounds of jazz partly to wrest the initiative from the white man, partly because they were sick of the elementary and unsubtle big-band style of their day, and partly because it amused them.

The darker side to all this was his drug addiction and its consequences. On his own admission Parker was 'hooked' at fifteen, and perhaps in an effort to escape he became an alcoholic at one time, habitually drinking eight double whiskies before starting a job. This mixture of drink and heroin, marijuana and benzedrine, together with a disregard of sleeping habits (he just passed out sometimes) made him too great a professional risk for regular employment. In the end, instead of consorting with his musical peers, he was doing gigs with any rhythm section he could get together.

Perhaps such a life could never be described coherently, and Mr Reisner is right to throw it at us, beat poems ('Bird = a god of good graciousness') and all, so that we can construct our own version of this extraordinary Negro whom his acquaintances depict as a kindhearted bully, an honest cheat, a chess-playing satyriast. Or we can concentrate on that sentence of his reported by Al Cotton: 'Keep the bandstand like it was a sandpit —clean.' That, after all, is what the records are still saying.[45]

Guardian, 6 September 1963

21
Timbres Varied

DINOSAURS IN THE MORNING: 41 PIECES ON JAZZ by Whitney Balliett (Phoenix House, 15s)

SWING PHOTO ALBUM 1939 by Timme Rosencrantz (Scorpion Press, 21s)

I have always imagined that Whitney Balliett, jazz critic of the *New Yorker*, evolved his style after a careful study of the manner of his erstwhile colleague, the late A. J. Liebling.[46] For just as Liebling enriched his ambling, acute descriptions of the 'Sweet Science of Bruising' with sudden comical pictorial effects (Walcott 'flowed down like flour out of a chute,' Turpin's 'jab was like a man starting his run for the pole vault'), Balliett concentrates on what jazz music *sounds* like, what jazz musicians *look* like. He has discarded Liebling's broader human passages with taxi-drivers and fight managers, freed his technique of simile from its comic allegiances, and broken clean away from other jazz writers by reason of his conscious intention to make his prose as exciting as the music it deals with. Consider the following passage:

> This Basie rhythm section was the classic proof of the powers of implication, for it achieved its ball-bearing motion through an almost Oriental casualness and indirection, as if the last thing in the world it wanted was to supply rhythm for a jazz band. The result was a deceptive sailing-through-life quality that was, like most magic, the product of hard work and a multi-layered complexity that offered the listener two delightful possibilities: the jointless sound of the unit as a whole, or, if one cared to move in for a close-up, the always audible timbre of each of its components. And what marvellously varied timbres they were! At

> the top was Basie's piano, which, though most often celebrated for its rain-drop qualities, attained its relaxed drive from a skilful pitting of right-hand figures against heavy left-hand chords. On the next rung came Greene, a peerless rhythm guitarist, whose Prussian beat, guidepost chords, and aeolian-harp delicacy formed a transparent but unbreakable net . . .

This seems to me not only entirely accurate writing with here and there ('jointless', 'Prussian') a touch of genius, but a celebration of its subject that makes you want to get out those old Brunswicks again. Balliett, like Liebling, profits by the supposed contrast between his own literacy and the subject of his articles. 'It's a compliment to jazz,' he wrote in his previous volume, *The Sound of Surprise*, 'that nine-tenths of the voluminous writing about it is so bad,' but it is a compliment he himself withholds. A graduate of Cornell, a one-time poet, Balliett has devised an approach which, he hopes, 'at least breathes on the aesthetic mysteries of the music.'

This volume, a collection of *New Yorker* pieces covering 1957–62, shows pretty clearly the method's limitations. Concede at once that the writing, despite some floaters (Bix's tone was 'a carillon playing on a dry morning, an August moon over the water'), is an almost constant delight: what remains? Certainly Balliett, who lists as a hobby 'Blues, in the key of C only,' makes little attempt to tell us what the musicians are doing technically. The brevity of his record or concert review form precludes sustained examination of the music's historical or sociological bases. His interviews (Ida Cox, Ornette Coleman) lack the immediacy that would lead one to quote them as 'the undoctored incident that actually occurred.' There remains a charity, a hospitality of taste, that welcomes practically everything.[47] 'The beauties of Louis Armstrong and Red Allen in 1933, the Basie band of 1938, the Ellington band of 1940–42, Charlie Parker, Dizzy Gillespie and Sidney Catlett in 1945, and Mingus, Coleman and John Lewis now are equal and quite dissimilar. Listeners blind to this don't know what they're missing.' In the whole of this book I have found hardly a trace of hostility—he is a little repressive about Buddy Rich, but only (Balliett is acutely sensitive to drummers) in comparison with his beloved Catlett.

This, in an age where 'criticism' has come to mean 'adverse criticism', is highly pleasing. The danger is that the second it relaxes from an utter determination to render the unique quality of each performer or perform-ance in a way that will be recognised indefinitely, it may fall into a wishy-washy essayist's *John O'London's* third leader manner, unsupported by personal preference or interpretation. This sounds ungenerous: Balliett is far and away the most perceptive of jazz writers. But once you have read his book you may see what I mean.

Swing Photo Album is a period piece, made up of the kind of studio publicity photograph or posed action shot that preceded the present-day use of high-speed film and 35–mm. cameras. Baron Timme Rosencrantz, one of the Thirties European pioneers, was responsible for their original publication, and when they first appeared their rarity made them exciting. Now those carefree stances, gleaming teeth and highlighted hair look supremely sad. Perhaps you don't know what Cleo Brown, Sterling Bose or the Mills Brothers looked like. But, if you are under thirty, do you care?

Spectator, 10 July 1964

22

Testifyin' to the Blues Tradition

CONVERSATION WITH THE BLUES by Paul Oliver (Cassell, 36s)

MUSIC ON MY MIND by Willie Smith (MacGibbon & Kee, 30s)

It was a brilliant idea of that British blues expert, Paul Oliver, to compile his *Conversation With The Blues* on the lines of the historical tessellation *Hear Me Talkin' To Ya*. During June–September 1960, he travelled through the South and West of the United States, seeking out blues singers, recording their reminiscences and songs, and taking photographs. This was a major operation clearly inspired by a love of and reverence for this powerful and fascinating folk tradition from which almost the whole of popular music is at present derived, and the result will undoubtedly become one of the few authoritative sources for information on the social background of the blues singer.

Of the 68 persons quoted (as in *Hear Me*, each speaker makes several contributions, as if taking up the cue from what has just been said), some are world-famous artists such as Muddy Waters, Lonnie Johnson, Victoria Spivey; others are relatively or absolutely obscure. Their testimonies are rich and variegated: sometimes a ghostly roll-call ('And then I run up against Tommy Jackson—he was Tony Jackson's first cousin, the guy that wrote "Pretty Baby"—he was a great musician. Sudan Washington was a great musician; Cooney Vaughans was one of the best piano players I ever heard and he was from Hattiesburg, Mississippi . . . '), sometimes anecdotal ('Well we got to Atlanty and we did all the drinkin' that day we were recordin'. We could have had ten gallons of whisky if we wanted. I say, "No

. . . I don't mind" when the bottle comes roun' '), sometimes speculative or philosophical ('Because there's some places in them records, there's somethin' sad in there that give you the blues: somethin' that reach back in your life or in some friend's life of yours, or that make you think of what have happened today and it is so true, that if it didn't happen to you, you still got a strong idea—you know those things is goin' on.') Great care has been taken to preserve the forms and rhythms of the speakers' words, and this deepens the impression of authenticity.

As Mr Oliver points out in his introduction, it is no longer possible to define the blues in terms of one particular performance or audience. The blues that were the half-muttered, half-hollered outcome of back-country misery and exploitation have little in common with the commercial success of rhythm and blues celebrities today. In the last contribution in the book the pianist Edwin Pickens reiterates what other singers say on the first page: 'The only way anyone can ever play the blues—he's got to have them. You got to have experienced somethin' in life. You been troubled, you been broke, hungry, no job, no money, the one you love is deserted you—that makes you blue. Blues makin' up his mind: "I'm gonna sing the blues." He's got to have a feelin' . . . ' This is no doubt partly true. More stress, however, might have been laid on the two faces of the blues—blues as sadness, and blues as excitement to escape that sadness.[48] Pickens's words seem to apply to the first mood only, and it may be significant that the popular blues modes today are mainly based on the second. In the last analysis, too, the very authenticity of the contributions makes for a certain monotony: anyone expecting Wordsworthian memorability will be disappointed. It makes me wonder whether *Hear Me Talkin'* may not have benefited by sub-editing.

Certainly one of its recurrent pleasures was quite different explanations by Willie 'The Lion' Smith of how he got his soubriquet. In *Music on My Mind* he opts for the First World War gun-crew version ('Smith, you're a lion with that gun') without alternatives. Nor are they crowded out by more colourful improbabilities: this book, rather to my surprise, is not unduly pretentious in tone, not one tall story after another. True, 'The Lion,' who at 67 is one of the few old-style pianists, insists that he used to give Jelly Roll Morton lessons at the keyboard—which, if you can believe, you can believe anything. In the main, however, he writes forthrightly, at times harshly, but with humanity, colour, and a certain mysticism on more recondite matters such as astrology, Judaism, and how to handle the booze. Or perhaps one should say this is how he talks, since the penwork was done by George Hoefer.[49]

This rambling, convoluted account of his life from the saloons of Newark, NJ, through the Field Artillery, Pod's and Jerry's, the Central Plaza, and finally the Newport Jazz Festival underlines not the romance and excitement of the jazzman's life but the discomfort and disillusionment. To play the piano from nine until dawn on an endless succession of drinks but no food, to have to repay part of your salary as a condition of getting union rates, to sit on cellar bandstands with your neck jammed against the ceiling—such trials call for self-discipline and self-respect, the tougher the better. 'The Lion's' discography proves that he endured them through five decades. One is left feeling that it has been a pretty good life none the less.

Guardian, 30 April 1965

23
Lovely Gigs

OWNING UP by George Melly (Weidenfeld & Nicolson, 30s)

I could never watch (the verb is chosen advisedly) George Melly singing without feeling embarrassed, and the same goes for reading this book. He is so anxious to tell you which birds he had it off with, what character's armpits smelled like the hallway of a cat-infested slum, and who peed in a washbowl where someone else had left a lettuce to soak that, free speech or not, one soon wishes he would belt up. It's not so much an adolescent desire to shock (though that element is there) as an adolescent sense of humour. On page 37 he dismisses one of his cast as 'overfond of the idea that eight pints of beer and a loud fart were insignia of the free spirit,' seemingly unaware that a similar two-barrelled sentence, differently loaded perhaps, could be turned on himself. Four-letter words pop like crackers on Guy Fawkes' night.

For students of the jazz scene in this country, however, there is much to be learned from it. Melly, as most of his readers will know, sang with the Mick Mulligan band throughout the fifties, and the value of his account lies in the picture he gives of how jazzmen actually earned a living at that time rather than in any perception of trends. It is an oddly innocent world: nobody takes drugs, or is an alcoholic, or needs more than a few hours sleep to be up and at it again. Even Melly's view of it is innocent, for gradually one realises that for him, in consequence of his nannie and public school background, sweaty socks and appalling lodgings and body-lice are romantic ('I had hopes of squalor on an heroic scale'). Its keynote is energy—the energy of the simple Spanier-type music, the energy required to drive back to London night after night in the small hours after each engagement, the energy to keep drinking.

Beyond the chaos of anecdotes (and some, to be fair, are quite funny, such as the royal portrait inscribed 'Lovely digs, Mrs Flanagan—Liz and Phil') one discerns from time to time glimpses of the London scene—the rise and fall of trad, the brief reign of Tommy Steele, Barber, Bilk and Ball, visiting firemen such as Broonzy, Rushing and Rosetta Tharpe. At Easter, 1963 he helps compère a big BBC show at the Albert Hall and notes that the stars of the evening 'were a group I'd only just heard of'—John, Paul, George, and Ringo, no less. At the close of the book he can walk past a queue of several hundred blues fans at The Marquee and not be recognised—this after falling off the stage during 'Frankie and Johnny' for eight years. *Tout lasse, tout casse, tout passe.*

Perhaps it is as a portrait of a band that the book is most successful: Melly is very good at describing the genesis and development of the kind of asinine group-joke that becomes a routine or cliché in the fatigued early hours—for instance, the 'points' game, or the teasing of personalities. The Mulligan team was noted for this kind of lark, and to some extent resemble the Condon crew described some ten years earlier in *We Called It Music*. The difference is that whereas Condon made you want to be one of his crowd, Melly makes you profoundly grateful you're not.[50]

Guardian, 29 October 1965

24
Didn't They Ramble

FOURTEEN MILES ON A CLEAR NIGHT by Peter Gammond and Peter Clayton (Peter Owen, 25s)

Some five years ago I made a plea on this page for a *belle-lettriste* of jazz, a Newman or Cardus, who could chat amiably about the music without feeling they had to do the up-the-river-from-New-Orleans stuff every time they opened a typewriter. Now Messrs Gammond and Clayton have the same idea, claiming that they have written the equivalent of 'Rambles Round My Shelves' and other examples of pleasant literary waffle, as they call it. Is this what I meant?

Far from it. What Gammond and Clayton (names to be respected in the field of jazz journalism) have done is write forty-odd free association pieces about as many records, plus some more bits not about records, and collect some quotations illustrated by pen and ink drawings signed 'P.' The prevailing tone is one of unrelenting facetiousness, e.g. (of 'Squaty Roo') *'Squaty* from the Old French esquatir, meaning to flatten, and *Roo* from an old English book called "Winnie-the-Pooh," meaning a small kangaroo. Hence—a small flattened kangaroo. Very curious really, because at first hearing the music does not suggest this at all—nor at any subsequent hearings, for that matter.' Now if anyone finds that funny, they had better rush off with their twenty-five bob to the nearest bookseller, because this is their book: it is nearly all like that.

The funny thing is that the 40 records they choose as vehicles are particularly magnificent examples of recorded jazz, and the best use of the book (apart, as the authors might have said, from propping up your Aunt Fanny's aspidistra stand) is simply as a list of tracks you must hear. The prevailing taste is traditional or mainstream—I counted a 33 to 7 split against the moderns—but none the worse for that, and it is remarkable how often the authors hit on a piece that at least one reader thought he was probably a little eccentric for treasuring—Muddy Waters's 'Louisiana Blues,' for instance, or Bechet's 'Nobody Knows The Way I Feel Dis Mornin'.' Miff Mole's 'Alexander's Ragtime Band,' Noone's 'Four or Five Times,' and Hampton's 'Twelfth Street Rag' are other examples unerringly selected by what one feels must be impeccable taste.

But what happens to this taste when the authors begin to write? To be fair, it must be admitted that they occasionally produce a good line: Muddy Waters's guitar 'glints menacingly like gun-metal'; a Mojo is 'a sort of Negro Joan the Wad'; 'Yancey's Blues' 'seems as packed as one of those seconds said to be experienced by a dying man.' Perhaps the average reader will find others. After all, the authors apologise to the critics 'who are going to be deeply hurt by it all.'

Guardian, 20 May 1966

25
Very Good Friend

Fats Waller's face, 14 versions of which appear on the cover of Ed Kirkeby's *Ain't Misbehavin'* (Peter Davies, 35s), was the kind you can carve on an orange; squeeze it one way and it laughs, another and it weeps or looks puzzled. This battery of expressions was part of his stock-in-trade as an entertainer, for the cheerful little earful, or harmful little armful (he weighed a steady twenty stone) was in the laughter business as much as the jazz business. Like many fat people, he soon discovered that the way to prevent people laughing at him was to make them laugh with him; when he had their attention he could dominate them with his powerful virtuoso playing.

One looks to his first full-length biography to see what, if anything, lay behind this life-long façade. Ed Kirkeby managed Fats for the last five years of his life: the last forty pages or so are based on his personal diary, but for the first 13 chapters he presumably draws from Duncan P. Scheidt and Sinclair Traill, who are billed as collaborators. Perhaps in consequence the book lacks the focus of an integrated view of the subject; the character of Fats as a roaring boy, a jazz version of Dylan Thomas or Brendan Behan, is accepted without much query. From his early days as Wurlitzer organist at New York's Lincoln Theatre to the last engagement in Hollywood, Fats was perpetually having a ball; he was the kind of person parties start up around with almost gruesome relentlessness. On getting up in the morning, he took four fingers of whisky ('my liquid ham and eggs'), followed by another four fingers when he had shaved. At recording sessions he invariably had a quart on the piano and another quart in reserve. About women the account is more reticent, but 'cute chicks' appear sufficiently frequently to suggest that Fats denied himself little in this way also. When Mr Kirkeby finally got him on the train after his illness in Los Angeles and several consecutive all-night all-day parties to mark his departure from the Zanzibar Room, fresh gaiety arose when he entered the club car. By the time the train had reached Kansas City, Fats was dead. He was 39.

Three extenuating qualities can be discerned from this anecdotal and not particularly distinguished account of his life. First, people loved him: Kirkeby, meeting him after twenty years in the recording business, recalls that 'the great round brown face smiled across at me, and I knew that, without the slightest doubt in the world, here was a man I would love to the end of my days.' This enormous charm surmounted his unpaid debts, broken contracts, neglected alimony, betrayed wives: at his funeral ten thousand people listened to the Rev. Adam Clayton Powell Jr.,[51] and traffic was stopped for three blocks. After his death, Louis Armstrong said 'Every time someone mentions Fats Waller's name, why, you can see grins on all the faces.' Groups of friends, meeting to console each other for their loss, ended by roaring with reminiscential laughter.

Secondly, he was a natural musician. As a jazz pianist he stands between James P. Johnson, who taught him, and Art Tatum, who learnt from him, but it is he who has the greatest variety of mood, from feather-light whimsicality to the solid springing tenths in the left hand that never let the rhythm falter for a moment.[52] A facile composer, he could turn out a ballad practically on demand in exchange for whisky, hamburgers or 'trash': on July 17, 1929 he sold Irving Mills 19 numbers (including 'Ain't Misbehavin' ') for $500, less than a good week's salary.[53] The casual little records he made in the thirties ('My Very Good Friend The Milkman,' 'When Somebody Thinks You're Wonderful') have outlasted more ambitious works, and are still played on Housewives' Choice.[54]

Lastly, one closes the book feeling that for all his success there was a part of Fats that had lost its way and wanted to go home. His father had been an Abyssinian Baptist pastor and his mother had helped in the services: Tom, as Fats was christened, had played the organ. Throughout his life, hymns and spirituals on a Hammond or Wurlitzer indicated that his deeper feelings were involved; in the small hours (Waller hated to sleep alone) he would announce 'Now for my favourite tune . . . ' It proved to be 'Abide With Me,' one of his mother's songs. She had died when Fats was sixteen, and his unhappy first marriage had immediately followed. Towards the end of his own life, Kirkeby reports elsewhere, he composed a melody that so 'shook his soul' that he could never find words good enough to fit it. The title gave him no difficulty, though. It was 'Where Has My Mother Gone?'

Guardian, 8 July 1966

26
Soul Food

URBAN BLUES by Charles Keil (University of Chicago Press, 37s)

It's a common contention among present-day jazz writers that the blues have fallen on evil times. In place of the nobility that informed the classicism of Bessie Smith, the hesitant off-pitch originality of the country singers, and the astonishing versatility of such walking compendia as Leadbelly and Big Bill Broonzy, we have numerous spruce-haired young men turning up the volume of their electric guitars and whanging out a series of indistinguishable numbers, varied only by the occasional excursion into lachrymose or hysterical sentimentality. Such a view, however, Mr Keil finds anathema: it is 'a semi-liberal variant of the patronising "white man's burden" tradition that has shaped white attitudes towards Negroes for centuries ... There is also an escapist element ... By concentrating on old-timers and scorning today's blues as commercial or decadent, the writer can effectively avert his eyes from the urban ghetto conditions that spawn the contemporary forms.'

Mr Keil's standards seem, basically, sociological: the blues—urban, soul, rock and roll, rhythm and blues, the whole spectrum—are good because they unite their audience in a way comparable to the church service, which in some ways they resemble. A singer such as B. B. King becomes a cultural hero through dealing with the conflicts and tensions of his hearers; a Bobby Bland show (one is fairly closely described) is 'a simple and direct way of dramatising solidarity and the basic idea that we're all in this thing together.' What thing, the reader may ask? Why, the Negro question, the racial problems of America, Watts, Alabama, the lot, and it is obviously Mr Keil's aim to paint modern Negro urban culture as something tough and independent of white criticism.

His qualifications for doing so are academic training, presumably in the social sciences, at Yale, Indiana and Chicago, and experience as a jazz musician: he is also, one assumes, a Negro, a friend and follower of the late Malcolm X (to whom the book is dedicated), and sufficiently at home in the world he writes about to interview B. B. King backstage and attend a Chess recording session with Little Milton Campbell. All the same, his book is not wholly convincing. It suffers in places from inflated academicism, repetitiveness, and lack of connected argument, and the fact that all the sociological justification in the world isn't going to make the 'refined' blues that is the speciality of this mode ('no harps, moaning or stuff like that') any more impressive as jazz music.[55]

The presentation of the blues-man as a 'culture hero' is rather difficult to evaluate. Mr Keil clearly feels that these artists are worthier of attention in this role than, say, Gracie Fields or Sir Harry Lauder, and the key chapter on this is 'Soul and Solidarity,' which reaches the conclusion that B. B. King and the rest 'are the incarnations of soul; they do transform the collective "mind" into representative activities. A good blues lyric is a representative anecdote, the distillation of a problem, the naming of a malaise.' M'yes. They no doubt work hard as entertainers ('This is an "ass-kissing" business') and employ 'solidarity' techniques ('I want everybody to raise their right hands and repeat after me, "I hereby bear witness to the blues!" '), but the samples of their work quoted by Mr Keil are sometimes dismaying:

> Soft tears that I shed for you,
> The little favours that I loved to do,
> The quick response to your every call,
> Oh, darlin', oh, darlin', you're worth it all.

Personally, I should rate George Formby's 'Chinese Laundry Blues' well above this, as soul, solidarity, and even jazz.

When Mr Keil reports directly on the blues world he is enlightening: the recording session and the account of the bluesman's career are interesting and acute. Above this level, however, he tends to wobble, as on page 154 where the bluesman is credited with greater vocational 'specialisation' than 'the President of the United States, Albert Schweitzer, the dedicated priest . . . ' Perhaps the assertion is justifiable, though, in a context where even bowling with the boys has 'the non-avocational aspect of increasing group solidarity'.

Guardian, 7 October 1966

27
Gulliver's Travails

SHADOW AND ACT by Ralph Ellison (Secker & Warburg, 42s)

This collection of essays, interviews, and reviews, diverse though its impact necessarily is, has a curiously original ring at this moment. It is the chippings and shavings from the work of a writer who *happens*—and here the cliché is really applicable—to be an American Negro.[56] The originality lies in the fact that although he recognises the singular role his race has at present ('I propose that we view the whole of American life as a drama acted out upon the body of a Negro giant, who, lying trussed up like Gulliver, forms the stage and the scene upon which and within which the action unfolds'), he is not really interested in his Negro characteristics, compared with his heritage as a man and an artist. Ellison was 'freed' not by the Negro Freedom Movement but by Marx, Freud, T. S. Eliot, Pound, Gertrude Stein and Hemingway: 'It requires real poverty of the imagination to think that this can come to a Negro *only* through the example of *other Negroes.*'

This may be due in part to his being born in Oklahoma, where by his own account there was no tradition of slavery and relations between the races were more fluid and human than in the old slave states. 'By early adolescence the idea of Renaissance Man had drifted down to about six of us . . . ': when he began to write, under the tutelage of Richard Wright,[57] he found the latter 'overcommitted to ideology'. Paradoxically, however, he does not side with Wright about the 'essential bleakness' of the Negro's life in America: he wants 'to affirm those qualities which are of value beyond any question of segregation, economics or previous condition of servitude . . . all Negroes affirm certain feelings of identity, certain foods, certain types of dancing, music, religious experiences, certain tragic attitudes towards experience . . .'. Compared with that of the white Southerner, the Negro's life is rich—a contention somewhat at odds with the Black Power platform.

One wonders whether this has anything to do with his early experiences of jazz music. As a youngster he 'hung around the old Blue Devils orchestra,' that remnant of the Moten band from which the second greatest large jazz orchestra in history, the Basie group, was fashioned, and for a long time tried to be a musician. This sudden flashpoint of what came to be known as Kansas City jazz was an artistic explosion as great in its own way as anything Paris had in the twenties, and one can tell by the way Ellison recurs to it that he recognises the deep impression it made on him.

Of the now-celebrated Jimmy Rushing, whose voice he could hear four blocks away from Slaughter's Hall over the incessant noise of freight from the Rock Island roundhouse, he writes: 'He expressed a value, an attitude about the world for which our lives afforded no other definition.' He remembers Lester Young in 1929, sitting jamming in Halley Richardson's shoeshine parlour in Oklahoma City, head back, feet working on the footrests, and the effect he had on a boy who was in the same class as the writer's young brother, one Charlie Christian,[58] who spent much of his school life manufacturing guitars from cigar-boxes in the manual-training department. Such encounters with men destined to become world-famous could well be the key to his whole social philosophy.

Guardian, 13 January 1967

28
Disagreeable to Unbearable

THE JAZZ CATACLYSM by Barry McRae (Dent, 30s)

The jazz historian is usually either a Wells or a Gibbon:[59] either things are growing better and better, or they are getting progressively worse. Since the music seems to be suffering a radical upheaval every twenty years, there is plenty of evidence for either side.

Mr McRae is a whole-hearted Wells, and his book is designed to elucidate the last great jump forward, from Parker to Ornette Coleman and free form. He begins with the 'cooling' of the bop revolution ('Although it arrived as a conscious rebellion against a stereotyped music, it began to suffer from just this trouble itself'), and studies in turn all the growth points of the fifties—Mingus, the Messengers, soul, Coltrane, and Rollins. Finally he arrives at Ornette Coleman, about whom he has no reservations. Coltrane and Davis had prepared the way with their experiments with modality: Coleman 'was not only the first man to affect free form in jazz ... he was the first to provide the style with a valid grammar of its own ... The discoveries made by Coleman in the last decade will become part of the fabric of jazz as surely as did those of Armstrong, Morton, and Parker.' And after Coleman comes Charles Lloyd, Ayler, Shepp, Tchicai; the torch is being handed on, and Mr McRae sees the future of jazz as an even greater expressionism, a music of the psychoanalyst's couch.

This account of jazz in the last twenty years is thorough and readable, backed up with a discography and the advantage of having talked personally to many of the players whose work it describes. Mr McRae's judgments of jazzmen are always made with reference to their vitality and genuineness; he is aware of the opportunities for the charlatan that a revolution in any art provides, and thinks he can distinguish, so to speak, the Shepps from the goats. The unaffected, considered way in which he writes persuades the reader of the soundness of his position.

The only criticism one can make of the book is that it gives no suggestion to the reader that the Gibbons of jazz would think it wrong from start to finish. The pinched neurosis of bop was bad enough; the absurd cacophonous hostility of the New Thing is excruciating. Mr McRae's last words, 'the free form players retained the blues as the lifeblood of their art,' are to my ears, grotesque. His suggestion seems to be that, after a few hearings, Coleman is not much different from Parker or even Armstrong. It would certainly be nice if he wasn't. But he is.[60]

Guardian, 7 July 1967

29
Jazzmen

FOUR LIVES IN THE BEBOP BUSINESS by A. B. Spellman (MacGibbon & Kee, 36s)

This is an absorbing book in more ways than one. Primarily it is an account of the careers and aims of four jazzmen—not, in fact, beboppers, despite the quaintly period title—who have made, or tried to make, the scene in the last decade or so. But it is also a study of the artist in society under conditions which have virtually disappeared from the other arts—the jazzman, in other words, is still socially unacceptable, and forced to sell his art as entertainment; if he cannot do this, there are no Arts Council bursaries or Creative Writing fellowships for him to fall back on. Throughout Mr Spellman's pages there runs a savage sense that in this world dedication to one's art really means something in terms of suffering.

These four American Negroes—Cecil Taylor, Ornette Coleman, Herbie Nichols, and Jackie McLean—are, or were (Nichols died in 1963), men who incurred hostility in three ways: they were Negroes, they were jazzmen, and they were *advanced* jazzmen. 'When the group got there, we found he had left a Negro manager in charge who seemed to feel that his music was not good enough for the Coronet. After the first set he contacted Cecil and told him he was fired. He just said, "We don't want this music in here, you're fired." Cecil was very hurt, very dragged ... His first thought was to shield his saxophone case in both arms, and he tried to hide his face behind the case. They pried his arms apart, smashed his case, smashed the saxophone, and threw it off the hill. Then they threw Ornette down, and kicked him.'

This is the kind of reaction their music could provoke. In what way was it advanced? In the same way that any 'modern' art is advanced: by dispensing with all conventions hitherto thought to be necessary—in this case, tune, key, harmony, pitch.[61] Altoist Jackie McLean remembers Charlie Mingus telling him, ' "Forget about changes and forget about what key you're in," and "All notes are all right," and things like that, and it kind of threw me.' They were all seeking the 'something else' Charlie Parker had postulated: 'there's got to be something else.' Ornette Coleman made an LP of this title.

In consequence the book is also about economics and artistic compromise. Perhaps the saddest story of the four is that of Herbie Nichols, a pianist with a style somewhere between Teddy Wilson and Thelonious Monk, who seemed fated to earn a living playing the most retrospective Dixieland in dives where Ivy League students 'would come in with their trombones, clarinets and crew-neck sweaters, surround Herbie, and call "When The Saints Go Marching In".' Near the end of his life he told the author 'I'm not making $60 a week ... I wish I could get some African government, Ghana, for instance, interested in my music and give me a job teaching ... ' Ornette Coleman expresses himself bitterly on the subject of economic discrimination: 'I've never gotten $2,000 a week yet. The most I've gotten is $1,200 a week. And yet I've packed audiences into the same clubs that have been paying $4,000 a week to people who haven't packed the house ... This is the worst kind of suffering, this psychological suffering of knowing you're being exploited.' The complaint that record manufacturers refuse to disclose details of sales, or make more than token payments, occurs in more than one section.

Mr Spellman is himself a Negro, and there is no doubt that his book is slanted to make you feel that these men have been treated pretty disgracefully, which is certainly true to some extent. Beyond this, however, one faces the question of how far society should pay an artist for doing something society doesn't want doing, or how the pioneers of any 'new thing' are to live before it catches on and somebody—usually not them —makes a mint.[62] Mr Spellman's book, which is admirably produced by transcribing tape-recordings, so that much of the text carries the natural rhythms of his subjects' voices, shows that the bebop business is no better at providing the answer than one might expect.

Spectator, 11 August 1967

30
The New Yorker Beat

SUCH SWEET THUNDER by Whitney Balliett (MacDonald, 35s)

Whitney Balliett joined the *New Yorker* in 1951, a few weeks after leaving Cornell (where he took a degree in English), and has been writing jazz features for them since 1957. By now, naturally enough, his style is well-known. He belongs to the *reportage* school of criticism, in which at least half the writer's talent goes into making you *hear* or *see* the cricket, the boxing, the jazz. Here, for instance, is Gene Krupa:

> When he played, his hair fell over his eyes; he chewed gum; he hunched over his drums or reared back, his arms straight in the air, like a politician at a rally; he sweated; in his climactic moments he converted his arms and hands and drumsticks into sculpted blurs.

Fair enough, you think. But what about what he is actually doing?

> He might start with rapidly swelling and subsiding rolls on the snare (accented here and there on the rims), break into an irregular pattern of rimshots mixed with tom-tom beats, press into an even, multi-stroked roll, pass his way with greater and greater speed through half a dozen rudiments, and close with staccato rimshots. He didn't bother to adjust his volume and he rarely paused, not realising that silences in drum breaks are twice as stunning as a mounting roar.

If anyone thinks he can produce a better description of a Krupa drum solo than that, he is welcome to try. The prose, it will be noticed, is literate without being literary; Balliett is at home with the technical term ('rudiments') as well as with the sharp image ('like a politician at a rally'), but he keeps these things in hand, subordinate to the job of saying what the music was like.

* * *

He is, of course, American: his beat is the clubs, the concerts, the recording studios, and the records of jazz America from 1962 to 1966. The pieces he produces can be four pages long or twenty: there are some excellent portraits-in-depth of Pee Wee Russell, Henry 'Red' Allen, Earl Hines, and Mary Lou Williams. After reading his 350-odd pages one has the impression of having spent the last four years in the US listening to jazz: one also has the inimitable experience of recognising one's records again in Balliett's prose. His chief characteristic, as a critic, is that he has virtually no characteristics: in a potted biography published in 1959 it was said that Balliett 'professes equal interest in all types of jazz.'

This is probably the only charge that can be levelled against him: he has no blind spots. As Arnold Bennett said of Eddie Marsh, he's a miserable fellow, he enjoys everything.[63] He ranges from Ornette Coleman at the Village Vanguard to Kid Thomas at Preservation Hall, and one looks almost in vain for a barbed remark, much less for a hatred as vehement as one of his many delights.

In the end, too, one looks for background: Balliett's foregrounds are wonderful, Zutty Singleton's gentle, teddybear face, the peaks and cloud kingdoms and heavenly pastures in Armstrong's playing, Giuseppi Logan's violin solo 'made up of a million short, scratchy notes,' but where is jazz going; what is happening to the American Negro, why are we in a concert room instead of the dance hall? No doubt Balliett could write on these things, but in the event he doesn't, and we are left in the end with an impression of brilliant superficiality. Perhaps this is editorial policy: the *New Yorker* was always strong on polish. But the only thing you can polish is a surface.[64]

Guardian, 29 March 1968

31

Byways of the Blues

SCREENING THE BLUES by Paul Oliver (Cassell, 42s)

'It is one of the strengths, but also one of the weaknesses of the blues,' writes Mr Oliver, 'that—' well, to put it bluntly that it attracts performers who can neither play nor sing. And, in fact, one does get heartily sick of the blues at times: the whimpering and mumbling about 'my baby done lef' me,' the kindergarten smut, the outmoded proprieties ('Please, Mr Fireman'), and above all the relentless lack of originality; for thirty or forty years we have had to endure these same icemen and riders and back doors and evening suns going down.

Mr Oliver admits this: as he says, the 'stockpile of traditional phrases' serves as 'an indispensable substitute for original thought.' The blues has nothing of the calypso's vitality; 'national events and successes are seldom recorded; political comment is to be found on a handful of blues, Jim Crow laws and poll taxes hardly at all. Of the Civil Rights movement, of freedom marches, of anti-segregation demonstrations and lunch-counter sit-ins, Black Muslims and Black Power, the blues says nothing.' Not even about lynching.

Nevertheless, the music has its devotees, and Mr Oliver is one of them. The present book reads rather like a lengthy footnote to his earlier book *Blues Fell This Morning*, published in 1960; this was a moving tessellation of blues lyrics and exegetical comment arranged to show what the main themes of the blues were—work, railroads, love, and so on. *Screening the Blues* takes up half a dozen minor blues themes, Christmas, preaching and preachers, the numbers game, Joe Louis, and obscenity, illustrating them in much the same way from historical records.

These are interesting enough, though to say that Negroes regard Christmas as a week-long debauch or that they suspect preachers of having an eye for drink and women is hardly to demonstrate that their society is utterly alien to ours. Even the chapter entitled 'Policy Blues,' with its exposition of the widely-popular 'numbers racket' organised by mobsters such as Dutch Schultz, has not basically a greater emotional appeal than a group of blues based on football pools. But the themes are knowledgeably and intelligently deployed, and add to our knowledge of Negro life.

Probably the final section, 'The Blue Blues,' will earn the book its keep: Mr Oliver has taken advantage of the present permissive climate in publishing to include a study nearly a hundred pages long of 'obscene' Negro blues and songs. These range from the innumerable metaphors ('Phonograph Blues'—'my needle point got rusty,' etc.) to much more outspoken conventions, such as 'Shave 'Em Dry,' and 'The Dirty Dozens,' an odd Negro insult game wherein each player utters outrageous abuse of the other's family, until one or other can stand it no longer and the knives come out.

Although blues singers are much bolder than normal about sex, to the extent of calling themselves Steady Roll Johnson or Boodle-It Wiggins, most blues lyrics are heavily censored by the record company, and what gets past is usually impenetrable under a strong accent. Mr Oliver has dug out several where the language is improper, but in most cases it sounds as if the singer was trying to shock, rather than make the audience supply the obscenity mentally, as in the large majority of the songs. The suggestion is that obscenity is the release of social tension, which the American Negro is well acquainted with, and so an agent of health. Certainly there is a wealth of material here that will come as a surprise to most blues followers.

The book, by the way, should really be read in conjunction with a record **Screening The Blues** (CBS 63288), which includes a number of the songs referred to, and which supplies the dimension of musical excitement as Mr Oliver's somewhat colourless prose never could.

Guardian, 6 September 1968

32
Unacknowledged Legislators

THE STORY OF THE BLUES by Paul Oliver (Barrie & Rockliff: The Cresset Press, 60s)

It is an irony almost too enormous to be noticed that the thorough penetration of Anglo-Saxon civilisation by Afro-American culture by means of popular music is a direct, though long term, result of the abominable slave trade. Anyone who has lived through the last 30 years will know that English popular music has been permeated, at first covertly and then openly, by the music of the American Negro, and in particular the blues, which, in the words of the present book, 'moved from the circumscribed world of a segregated minority to become the inspiration of popular music through society.'

Does this mean anything more than that our children sing one kind of music rather than another? It's hard to say. Someone said: 'Let me write a nation's songs, and anyone you like can make the laws,' by which I suppose is meant that the songs will show how people really behave, and may even condition the laws themselves; if this is true, then we may owe the permissive society to the Charleston. God knows what we shall be getting in 2009, when today's youth have become legislators.

It's an interesting speculation, but mine rather than Mr Oliver's, whose new book has a deceptive cannabis-table appearance, being of large format and largely pictorial content. This is because it is based on the 1964 American Embassy exhibition which, as those who saw it will remember, was largely made up of remarkable photographs in this particular field. Mr

Oliver has now added a serious and valuable text to go with the pictures, based more on the lives and personalities of the blues singers than—as at least two of his other books were—on what they sang.

I was not sure whether the plan of Mr Oliver's book was to follow the movements of the blues singers as a phenomenon—the end-papers are entitled 'Blues Centres and Recording Locations' and 'Migratory Routes' respectively—or whether he was employing a biographical method in chronological order. Sometimes he seems to be doing one, sometimes the other, and it's not an easy book to find one's way about in consequence.

Chain gangs

This is not to say it is not interesting: on the contrary, Mr Oliver presents a fascinating panorama of the medicine shows, country picnics, logging camps, chain gangs, and the bizarrely-named and semi-legendary figures that appeared at them, plucking a six or twelve-string guitar and singing what at times bordered on old field hollers, at times reported Negro social life, at times chronicled famous crimes or love affairs.

What kind of man was the blues singer? Usually a disability, more often than not blindness, debarred him from earning a living in the usual ways. Sometimes the itinerant life of the blues musician appealed to the temperament of a man capable of following it, or the discovery that he could earn money by playing at fish fries and the like, as well as by making records, led him to abandon his job as a farmhand or whatever it was. As a general rule, he didn't become as prosperous as the jazz man because he was earning at a much lower and more restricted level, and his wayward nature frequently led him to squander what money he received (Bessie Smith is a classic case in point).

Old slow blues

This, at any rate, was true of the old-time blues singer: Mr Oliver makes it clear that the gramophone record, and perhaps even more the radio station, played a dominant part in bringing about the blues boom, and the new technique of electrical amplification changed its character. Greater stress started to be laid on noise and speed, what Leadbelly called 'fast time and jump': 'If I was to stop playing the real old slow blues I don't know what would become of it'. This tendency was arrested to some extent by the rediscovery by antiquarians of the 'old-timers' such as Sleepy John Estes and Skip James, but this in turn was countered by the white invasion of the field (many Negroes went back to truck driving and general labouring rather than compete).

Mr Oliver's final paragraphs are written in the shade of present-day conditions: in our time, he says, the blues show 'every sign of cultural decline'—'the ascendancy of formal mannerism over content, the rococo flourishes and extravagant posturings both physically and instrumentally are signs of an art form in its final stages'.

It is certainly impossible to look at this impressive collection of photographs without thinking that the blues are to some extent dependent on poverty, misery and injustice, as inflicted on the American Negro, and that if this condition is to ameliorate—and in spite of many justified contemporary complaints, social circumstances for the Negro have greatly improved since the war—the blues may well decline and become extinct.[65] On the other hand, their dominance through blues-derived popular music shows no sign of diminishing. There is a contradiction here that it would be interesting to have resolved.

Editors' note: *Two photographs were printed in this review, bearing additional text:*

> Delta juke joint at Rome, Mississippi, typical of the places in that ravaged countryside where Son House sang and played the blues between the wars and killed a man on the rampage who had shot him in the leg. 'It's a dry ole spell, everywhere I been,' sang House: 'I believe to my soul this old world is bound to end' (from 'The Story of the Blues').

and

> Mugshot of Leadbelly (Huddie Ledbetter) whose criminal record listed: 'Homicide; Assault with intent to murder; Fel. Assault.' Sang Leadbelly: 'Never has a white man had the blues, 'cause nothin' to worry about.'

Guardian, 31 July 1969

33
Music to Stand up To

BLUES PEOPLE by LeRoi Jones (MacGibbon & Kee, 36s)

TALES by LeRoi Jones (MacGibbon & Kee, 30s)

Although the first of these two books will be meaningless to anyone ignorant of jazz, it is none the less basically a work of American sociology or political history.

Its purpose is to hail, expound and celebrate the sixties' avant-garde jazz of 'Ornette, Archie and Cecil' (Coleman, Shepp and Taylor), not primarily as music but (to quote Archie) 'a reflection of the Negro people as a social and cultural phenomenon . . . Culturally, America is a backward country, Americans are backward. But jazz is American reality. Total reality.'

Mr Jones, a Negro intellectual with a reputation in literature as well as jazz,[66] clearly sees the work of these men as something more than earning a living: 'It is expanding the consciousness of the given that they are interested in, not merely expressing what is already there, or alluded to. They are interested in the *unknown*. The mystical.'

In other words, 'black music' or the New Wave of the sixties is part of the general movement in America at present that causes, for instance, a Negro militant leader to stand up during a service in New York's Riverside Church and demand that American churches should pay his organisation $500 millions 'reparations,' for the part played by Christian churches in exploiting the Negroes.

This is something of a relief, for it was hard for anyone, even jazzmen themselves ('scream, rant, rave, blow horns, honk'—Shelly Manne) to see it as a kind of jazz. To see it as the musical equivalent of a flourished fist makes much better sense.

One has to accept that, for the moment anyway, the white American has got to take a good deal of this sort of thing from the Negro, who sees himself as (to quote Charlie Mingus) *Pithecanthropus Erectus*, the first man to stand upright. No wonder his music sounds a little excited and extravagant, and more than a little angry with those who kept him on all fours for so long.

Nor is it any use, now, offering a helping or comradely hand. Mr Jones disdains, in matters of pitch, 'the "precision" the Europeans claim with their "reasonable" scale which will get only the sounds of an order and reason that patently deny most coloured people the right to exist'—and this is his argument throughout.

So we have Ornette, Archie, and Cecil purveying a music that has jettisoned pitch, harmony, rhythm, in order to 'let out full to the heroic march spirituals and priestly celebrations of the new blackness.' This collection of rather fugitive essays, sleeve notes, and so on gives a scattered impression of why Mr Jones thinks it fulfils the role in which he has cast it: to him it is pure utterance, a life-attitude of energy, a cosmic comprehension, a new heaven and a new earth.

The passion with which he writes is moving rather than convincing, though at times one can see what he means: 'The new music . . . is "radical" within the context of mainstream America. Just as the new music begins by being free. That is, freed of the popular song. Freed of American white cocktail droop, tinkle, etc. The strait jacket of American expressions *sans* blackness . . . it wants to be freed of that temper, that scale. That life. It screams. It yearns. It pleads. It breaks out (the best of it) . . . '

In other words, the hideous racket these men produce is good not because it is music but because it expresses the political aspirations of some Negroes, of whom Mr Jones is one. This is why I call it a work of sociology rather than music criticism.[67]

Tales is much less interesting, a collection of short stories or pieces mostly dealing with Negro life in modern America. Written with violence rather than strength, their note of despairing aggression does not make for comfortable reading. Nor, I'm afraid, does it make for literature without other qualities of originality and organisation Mr Jones does not seem to possess at the moment.

Guardian, 4 September 1969

34

Jazz-Man's Sound and Fury

BENEATH THE UNDERDOG by Charles Mingus (Weidenfeld & Nicolson, £2)

Here at last is Mingus's autobiography. We've heard of it for nearly 10 years, and according to the sleeve he's been writing it for 20, so what is it like?

Predictably, it's like the man himself, muddled, violent, sophomore-sophisticated, suffering from elephantiasis of the ego, stylistically of the school of Baldwin and Burroughs, politically somewhere near LeRoi Jones (apart from the author's being related to Abraham Lincoln).

How interesting you find it depends on how much you like Mingus, the American Negro bass player who came up with Parker and Gillespie, getting his own groups together to churn out an individual brand of Holy-Roller modernism with titles such as 'The Black Saint and the Sinner Lady,' and constantly in the news for slugging his critics or sidemen or retiring from jazz altogether as a protest against white commercial supremacy.

Most of the book is in conversation, either with Mingus's analyst Dr Wallach or Fats Navarro, the late Negro trumpeter who died of t.b. in 1950, but there are many shadowy interlocutors who enable Mingus (so referred to, or 'Minkus,' 'my boy,' or 'Charles') to shoot his load of lust and rage, not to mention remorse and general bewilderment.

The book is inevitably light on dates, though we gather Mingus learned cello as a boy, switching to bass as a young man ('You're black. You'll never make it in classical music'), got married, separated, played with Lionel

Hampton, Lucky Thompson and Teddy Charles, indulged in sexual marathons, earned money by pimping, and after much flirtation with the psychiatrist's couch found himself 'inside' in earnest and threatened with frontal lobotomy, which caused reason to remount her throne pretty quickly.

The general impression it leaves is not unlike one of Mingus's own records: one recognises that the man *cares* tremendously, and is beating up a storm inside himself as well as outside, but all the time a still small voice is saying: Is this *really* original? Wouldn't it be *much* better cut by two-thirds? It's doubtful, in sum, if this book has a place in jazz literature. Put it among the literature of the American Negro, mid-century, X-certificate protest.[68]

Daily Telegraph, 26 August 1971

35
Satchmo Still

LOUIS: THE LOUIS ARMSTRONG STORY 1900–71 by Max Jones and John Chilton (Studio Vista, £3.20)

LOUIS ARMSTRONG: THE INTERVIEW by Richard Meryman (Eakins Press, New York: clothbound $4.95; card $2.95)

It's astonishing that a book as good as the first of these can be published so soon after Armstrong's death last July. The answer, of course, is that it is based on 'Salute to Satchmo,' by the same authors, that was published last year to commemorate Louis's seventieth birthday. All the same, I'm afraid you'll have to buy it. Max Jones's essay 'Seventy Years on the Throne' has been expanded to sixteen chapters; most of the original material is repeated, but a fat section (the middle ten chapters) now deals in remarkable depth with Oliver, Henderson, Russell, first European and 'Swing That Music' periods, and fascinating reading it makes. We learn, for instance, of Armstrong being 'busted' for dope in Los Angeles in 1931, and get his own philosophic summing up:

> Well, that was my life and I don't feel ashamed at all. Mary Warner, honey, you sure was good and I enjoyed you 'heep much.' But the price got a little too high to pay (law wise). At first you was a 'misdomeanor.' But as the years rolled on you lost your misdo and got meanor and meanor (Jailhousely speaking).

But a few words cannot convey the richness of illustration, fact, and anecdote this book contains.

It ends, rightly, on the note that, in spite of the world-wide recognition as an international figure, we may still be only on the threshold of understanding his true significance. Of course he was an artist of Flaubertian purity, and a character of exceptional warmth and goodness. But has anyone yet seen him as the Chaucer, say, of the culture of the twenty-first century? While we are wondering whether to integrate with Africa, Armstrong (and Ellington, and Waller, and all the countless others) has done it behind our backs.

The Meryman is a square-shaped book, the size of an EP,[69] and contains the 1966 *Life* interview without the questions.

Much of the ground is familiar, but it brings out afresh Louis's love for Joe Oliver, and how deeply his Henchardian[70] fate bit into Louis's view of life. Here was a great trumpeter who did not keep his chops in shape, who did not have a white manager:

> In 1937 my band went to Savannah, Georgia, one day—and there's Joe. He's got so bad off and broke, he's got himself a little vegetable stand selling tomatoes and potatoes. He was standing there in his shirtsleeves. No tears. Just glad to see us.

Nearly all the text has this compelling quality. It's something to do with the rhythm of the sentences ('Ain't but a few left, a few of us'), and something to do with the sentiments:

> But I always let the other fellow talk about art. 'Cause when we was doing it, we was just glad to be working up on that stage.

We have these books because Armstrong is dead. But their effect is to make his life seem just beginning.

Guardian, 21 October 1971

36
In Benny Goodman's Golden Days

The big band—a dozen or 14 young men in identical uniforms with creased trousers, their hair slicked and parted, set up behind ornamental music stands to play sweet numbers, comedy numbers and accompaniments to a glamorous, bare-shouldered 'vocalist' in an evening gown—is a thing of the past, not only economically but sociologically and musically as well.

The Big Bands (Collier-Macmillan, £2.75), a revised and enlarged edition of George T. Simon's 1967 book, accepts this: from the outset, he is a writer dealing with a historic phenomenon. The emotional core of his work is the brief decade between Benny Goodman's regular Saturday night coast-to-coast radio show in 1935 and the month of December 1946, in which no fewer than eight bands (including Goodman's, Herman's and Tommy Dorsey's) gave up.

This was 'the big band era,' when they 'were like big-league ball teams, and the kids knew all the players'; band leaders and their sidemen, in fact, got some of the adolescent adulation previously devoted to Hollywood personalities and familiar enough in our own day in the beat world. It came to an end when the draft began to bite and with Petrillo's 1942–44 ban on recording, and was succeeded, according to Mr Simon, by the Age of the Singer.

It follows that the bulk of this big book—385 out of 584 pages—is given over to accounts of 72 bands, most of which were riding high during this time. The bias is heavily white—only 12 bands were Negro—and some of the others—Dick Jurgens, Bobby Byrne—mean little today, if they ever did. The style is affectionate and anecdotal, carrying the flavour of *Metronome*,[71] where no doubt much of the material originated; there is a fair documentation of dates and line-ups, and plenty of official-seeming pictures, making everyone look incredibly young and decent.

The book might have been better had Mr Simon stopped there. Instead, he tags on nine more chapters into which are bundled ('The Horn-Playing Leaders . . . The Violin-Playing Leaders . . . ') everyone from Coon-Sanders to Spike Jones, and finally some 'revisited' chapters to catch the present views of Basie, Goodman, Shaw and a few other survivors.

Since these subsidiary mentions are brief, they add little to the reference value of the work, and indeed in general it rather falls between this all-inclusive status and being a great big hunk of American nostalgia. Underneath it all, too (for Mr Simon knows his scene), is the sense of exhausting dollar-dominated hysteria on which the big band floated. One is left feeling the book has size but not depth.

Daily Telegraph, 20 April 1972

37
Negroes of Europe

POP MUSIC AND THE BLUES by Richard Middleton (Gollancz, £4)

This book sets out to explain the most important cultural phenomenon since modernism: the take-over of world pop music by the American Negro. What is the secret of that seemingly inexhaustible form, the twelve-bar blues? Why must pop music be so loud and so frantic? Why do we instinctively know it's immoral?

Anyone who can answer such questions has a good deal to tell us about ourselves. Mr Middleton's approach is historical: he describes the blues and where they came from: country blues, city blues, soul. Then he moves on to pop, its evolution from the blues through rock 'n' roll, rhythm 'n' blues, and soul again, and its final emergence in the white groups. His treatment, however, is speculative: he calls the book 'the response of a musician to a musical phenomenon, and his attempt to unravel its meaning', but it is far from musicology in the ordinary sense:

> Pop is thus the climax of a long attempt to come to terms with non-Western experience through the Negro and his music.
>
> [The white adolescent] has created a new community—a classless, inter-national community, which is as real as any traditional group or class. A real change in values has manifested itself in a psychologically real, if practically rather would-be, change in social structure.

Les pauvres sont les nègres de l'Europe; for Mr Middleton it is *les jeunes*. Like the Negro, adolescents are trying to be free, and so form a conscious group seeking its own identity: their morality is 'specific, momentary and circumstantial.' Mr Middleton's obvious respect for those characteristics tempts one to add that neither group is very bright, either.[72] What has finally enabled them to fertilise each other, culturally, is the electronic revolution in communication, and this has also given the situation its international context.

One can't say this book is true or false, any more than one could of de Rougemont's *Passion and Society*: it interprets a set of circumstances and only time can show how convincingly. Mr Middleton is not an easy writer: musical and sociological jargon is thick on the page, and at times big style turns to melodrama ('after Robert Johnson the country style could not carry on ... For he had destroyed its basis ... the resulting trauma consumed himself').

Reference to Chilton's *Who's Who of Jazz* would have prevented him from repeating the exploded myth about the death of Bessie Smith. But he must be praised for having tackled a big and important subject, and the knowledge he brings to it should in itself ensure him a serious audience.

Guardian, 30 November 1972

38
Bessie & Billie

BESSIE by Chris Albertson (Barrie & Jenkins, £2.95)

LADY SINGS THE BLUES by Billie Holiday with William Dufty (Barrie & Jenkins, £2.95)

Three days after Bessie Smith had made her last recording in November 1933, Billie Holiday advanced nervously to the same microphone to make her first. Both were great jazz singers. Both had sad lives.

Up till now we have known little about Bessie, but Mr Albertson changes all that. Seeking out such key figures as her adopted son Jack Gee Jun., and her niece by marriage, Ruby Walker, he joins their testimonies to a mass of other original material to give a full-length portrait of his subject and a coherent narrative of her life. We follow Bessie from her teenage debut ('she just sang in her street clothes—but she was such a natural she could wreck anybody's show') through her success in the twenties, marriage to Jack Gee, the Depression, and her later association with Lionel Hampton's bootlegger uncle, Richard Morgan.

We learn she was a big, foul-mouthed, drinking woman, ready to make with her fists (she beat up Clarence Williams till he released her from a contract), whose sexual impulses turned as readily to the chorines in her road show as to any man. At the same time, she supported all her family (her three sisters drank as much as she did, without being able to sing), and was known as a soft touch: she also, as Van Vechten's photographs show, had a smile of marvellous radiance. Above all, she was a colossal artist, able to carry a show single-handed, and her Negro audiences adored her.

Bessie—or Miss Bessie, as you had to call her if you didn't want a smack in the chops—was a folk artist. When the blues lost out, she lost out with them: she didn't, like Alberta Hunter, tour with 'Show Boat,' or play to the Prince of Wales at the London Palladium like Ethel Waters. It took the Depression to change her repertoire; unfortunately there are no records of her singing 'Smoke Gets In Your Eyes' or 'Tea For Two,' but when John Hammond got her to Columbia in 1933 after a two-year lay-off the four magnificent songs she chose were none of them blues. It is heart-breaking that those were her last records, for she was better than ever. 'I feel I am on the brink of new successes,' she told a reporter in 1936. Next year she was dead, in the famous car crash.

Lady Sings The Blues was first published in 1958, and now appears unaltered to coincide with the film, plus a comprehensive discography by Albert McCarthy. Told in the first person, it is a much more bitter book: Bessie suffered when the tides of fashion and the economy ran against her, but she stayed with her people. Billie, competing in the white world, met segregation, narcotics and prison, and her music declined into the bargain. ('Nowadays you have all this talk and bull and nothing's happening.') Different in their styles, similar in their quality, these two women gave the world more than it could have ever repaid, even if it had tried.[73]

Guardian, 24 May 1973

39
Birdlife

BIRD LIVES! by Ross Russell (Quartet, £3.75 and £1.75)

Ross Russell, ex-President of Dial label, who once held Parker 'under what was laughably called an exclusive artist's contract,' was well qualified to do an authoritative life of him. This 'product of an obsession' draws on material found in 'areas rapidly becoming forbidden to the white man,' and constitutes a full-length in-depth study not only of Parker but of much of the post-war jazz world.

His theme is the development of the only jazz musician to equal Louis Armstrong, and his self-destruction by drug addiction, but the story is told with full attention to names, places, and financial details. After his apprenticeship in Kansas City, that jumpingest of jazz towns, Bird emerged as the presiding genius of the new inherently hostile Negro in-music of the Forties. Though Dizzy Gillespie got more work through being more reliable and socially at ease ('That's white of you,' he thanked an Ivy League helper), it was Parker who got the reverence, precisely because of his open reliance on heroin, his abandonment to sensation and the pleasure-principle, his complete disregard of moral and legal obligation.

But his reign lasted less than ten years. By the Fifties, bloated, badly dressed, he was doing one-nighters with a zombie rhythm section. When he died at 34, the certificate suggested four possible causes of death, and guessed his age at between 50 and 60.

Russell brings out well the 'Spoiled Brat' (he had a devoted and remarkable mother) view of Parker, and makes it clear that in spite of his ruthless dishonesty he could exert great charm and even humour. On his music he is less prepared to compromise: 'Louis changed all the brass players around, but after Bird all of the instruments had to change,' as Cootie Williams said. But was it for the better? Today much of Parker's febrile music seems good only insofar as it isn't as awful as what came after it. Not only Parker, but jazz, seems to have been bent on self-destruction.

Guardian, 28 June 1973

Editors' note: *this piece was headed by a photograph, under which appeared the additional text:*

Charlie 'Bird' Parker: 'ruthlessly dishonest,' but ' . . . after Bird all of the instruments had to change.'

40
Calling the Tune

IRVING BERLIN by Michael Freedland (W. H. Allen, £3.50)

Irving Berlin has been called the great primitive of American song-writing. 'I don't know anything about harmony,' he said in 1913, 'but I can make tunes.'

And that sums it up: this 'little man,' as Michael Freedland puts it, 'very intense, very jealous of his own reputation, very shy about himself, but very impressive,' wrote songs almost as easily as other men address envelopes—although 'wrote' is perhaps the wrong word: Berlin has never read or written music. He just produced tunes such as 'I'm Dreaming of a White Christmas,' 'What'll I Do?' and 'A Pretty Girl Is Like A Melody,' pieces that are not so much songs as bits of the twentieth century.

His early life was eventful. As Israel Blaine, he fled aged four with his Siberian Jewish parents to America in 1892. At 17, he was a singing waiter (oddly, in view of his uncertain tenor); at 23, he wrote 'Alexander's Ragtime Band,' after which, professionally at least, he never looked back.

His first wife died of typhoid five months after their wedding; his second was the daughter of a rich Roman Catholic who opposed the match. Berlin was soon richer than he was, however, and the opposition died away. After this his life became less eventful: hit followed hit, show followed show. Berlin's celebrated Army songs from the First World War ('Oh, How I Hate To Get Up In the Morning') were repeated ('This Is the Army, Mr Jones') in the second.

When in 1938 Katie Smith asked for 'a patriotic number,' he rehashed an old tune and called it 'God Bless America': he put the royalties in trust for American youth movements. He wrote a campaign song for Eisenhower, who later presented him with a special gold medal. Still unable to read music, he received an honorary Mus. Doc. from Bracknell University.

Berlin, now in his eighties, has never wanted his life written, a fact that may contribute to the two-dimensional quality of this one. All the same, something emerges: a sincere, modest, astute man who knew he had a gift but who didn't want to analyse it ('You can get too clever'). 'The mob is always right,' he insisted, which led him to write songs such as 'How Do You Do It Mabel on Twenty Dollars a Week?'. At the same time he was worried about his talent, especially during the Depression when he had to write to live.

'Perhaps the real dream job is being a failure,' he said wryly, 'then you wouldn't have to worry maintaining a standard.' On the other hand, despite his complete professionalism ('nobody steals songs, you understand—but there are only a certain number of song ideas'), he knew that the way to other people's hearts was through his own. As the *Encyclopaedia Britannica* said, 'his gift for simple, fresh melody won him instant popularity.'

There is no such thing as an Irving Berlin song, as there is, for instance, a Cole Porter song: there are simply 'Easter Parade,' 'It's A Lovely Day Tomorrow' and 'Say It With Music.'[74] But then, as Berlin said, 'You don't have to be different to be good. But if you're good, you're different.'

Daily Telegraph, 7 February 1974

41

That Nice Boy

BIX: MAN AND LEGEND by Richard Sudhalter and Philip R. Evans with William Dean-Myatt (Quartet, £4.95 and £1.95)

Early in February 1922, the Principal of Ferry Hall Girls' School wanted a band from the neighbouring Northwestern University to play at their dance. The leader, one Jimmie Caldwell, wanted to bring a trumpeter:

> I told her about this nice boy from Lake Forest, and how well-mannered he was, etc., and she said he would do . . . At the intermission [said Caldwell] the old girl grabbed me and marched me behind the palm plants. She said, 'That *nice boy* of yours is exciting my girls! Make him stop.' I told her he was playing what he felt and it would be hard to calm him down. 'Do it,' she said.

Bix Beiderbecke was 18 at the time and had 10 years to live, years in which he established himself as the greatest white jazzman and demolished himself with alcohol. Born in 1903 in a handsome tree-surrounded house in Davenport, Iowa, his prosperous German-American background seemed sufficient insulation against the rowdy dialect of Storyville, but in 1919 his ex-serviceman butler brought home some records, including the Original Dixieland Jazz Band's 'Tiger Rag'. Almost immediately Bix borrowed a cornet from a schoolmate. In August of the same year (for Davenport, after all, was on the Mississippi) he heard Armstrong on a riverboat with Fate Marable. In September he bought his own cornet for $35.

From then on, legend took over. The marvellous boy, self-taught and unable to read music, spiralled up through the campus dance field and into the Chicago jazz scene: no one who heard him ever forgot it. A dozen or so Gennett recordings with a home-grown group called the Wolverines led to the big time with Jean Goldkette's orchestra and, when Goldkette failed, to the biggest of all time, Paul Whiteman. His unique ringing sound, at once assertive and unworldly, became the voice of the WASP Twenties, the era of Gatsby and Julian English. After his death in 1931, legend fragmented into anecdote: even the records generated rumour and uncertainty. Which solo was by the master, which by one of his numerous pupils? Was Bix present, but too drunk to play? Could any more unissued test pressings possibly come to light?

Thorough documentation has long been overdue. The present work represents devoted research since 1957 by a distinguished and unselfish team of collaborators—Richard Sudhalter, journalist and cornet player in the Bix tradition, and two Bix scholars and discographers, Philip Evans in America and William Dean-Myatt in Britain. It is hard to think that anyone still alive who knew Bix has not been cross-examined, any date he played on not verified in the appropriate newspaper files, any extant building where he lived or played not reverently contemplated by one or other of this dedicated trio. Sudhalter, well-known in British jazz journals as 'Art Napoleon', did the writing, but his drafts were relayed to the others for checking and amplification. The result is an exhaustive 340–page life, with a 60–page day-to-day summary of Bix's musical and personal itinerary, and a 70–page discography, much fuller than anything easily available before.

It is fair to say that although the wealth of detail so assembled is nearly all unfamiliar, it doesn't substantially alter the legend as we know it. Bix was a genius: the *Davenport Democrat* called him, at seven, 'the most talented child in music that there is in this city'. He had perfect pitch and total musical recall: one of his tricks was to name each note in any ten-fingered chord you liked to strike. At the same time, he wouldn't, or couldn't, become a proficient reader: he had trouble getting into the union, and it was a measure of his renown that orchestras would engage him as 'featured soloist' (the legend of the Western novel open on his music desk is apparently well-founded). At times this worried him: when he approached Joe Gustat, the first-chair symphony trumpet declined to take him on. 'I envy you,' he said. 'You have a great, God-given gift . . . don't try to change it.' At the same time he said that Bix's fingering was 'all backwards', a verdict substantiated in detail by Sudhalter, who says that nonetheless it accounted for his explosive intonation.

The authors' somewhat hagiographical approach eschews 'revelations', but valuable reminiscence comes from Ruth Schaffner, whose affair with Bix is patiently documented. Though their relationship ultimately failed, she insists on his considerateness, his undeniable—even if rather absent —'niceness'. There is a typical story of his buying cigarettes when, a celebrity, he played on the Camel Hour programme. Bix didn't like Camels, but he always asked for them, then adding that he would also take a packet of the kind he really smoked.

On the central Bix question—whether he played with the wrong people, and ruined his talent by becoming a piece of jazz icing on the large, tasteless Whiteman cake—the authors are firm. A generous defence of the Whiteman orchestra asserts that Bix was in better musical company there than he would have been with

> less complex men such as Eddie Condon, Muggsy Spanier or Jimmy McPart-land. As his weeks with Whiteman stretched into months, he turned increasingly to the piano, and to the possibilities inherent in modern harmony.

Given a normal musical life, it's conceivable that he might have settled in the 'Rhapsody in Blue' territory, neither in jazz nor out of it, but whether he would have taken his admirers (of whom Condon was one) much of the way with him is doubtful. Nor is it easy to square this hypothetical Bix with his seeming indifference to musical theory. In any case, it was not to be. Little is said about his drinking, nor is there much to say: the authors suggest that he had passed from conviviality to addiction by October 1928, and after that the descent was steep. One element, again, was his niceness: he hated to say no. Another was surely the poisonous and uncertificated Prohibition booze. In the end he was drinking three bottles of gin a day. When the Depression lifted, Bix, and the world of white jazz he had inspired, were gone: the future lay with Goodman and his Henderson scores. Only the indestructible delight of his records remains.

New Statesman, 25 October 1974

42
Getting the Gigs

ALL THIS AND 10% by Jim Godbolt (Hale, £4.95)

MAHALIA by Alurraine Goreau (Lion Publishing, £1.95)

Had you realised that to bring together all these bands and groups on the one hand with all those corn exchanges and palais de dances on the other needs a separate sub-race of men called agents? I hadn't, but Mr Godbolt's book explains it all. What it doesn't explain is why he ever became one.

Originally a sensitive young man, loving his Miff Mole 78s and with a view about organic husbandry, he seems totally unsuited to the job of getting half-cut musicians back on to the stand, or making indignant or dishonest bookers pay up in full. He must have found it purgatory.

Starting after the war as 'general factotum' to George Webb's Dixie-landers, he was Mick Mulligan's agent from 1952 to 1961, then handled mainstreamers such as Bruce Turner, Fairweather-Brown and Wally Fawkes. Later he booked rock 'n' roll groups for a big multi-faceted organisation, his career thus covering most beat music fashions since the war. 'Around this thin heron-like figure,' as George Melly wrote in *Owning Up*,[75] 'a whole tradition of disaster has grown up,' and certainly the Lytteltons, Dankworths and Barbers always seem to be moving somewhere else; he even employed a man who once said, 'Mr Epstein, there are five thousand groups like that in London all looking for work.'

But the bands that stuck with him did so, one suspects, precisely because he lacked the mega-qualities that make the big time, having instead a certain decent quirky integrity ('although not, I like to think, without humour').

His 25–year survey of the British scene must be read for the worm's-eye detail it provides, and some of it is very funny in a sedate way ('Lyttelton's expression as he was referred to as an "employee" for the second time was worth seeing'). But in the end it is the revulsion one remembers: for the Musicians' Union ('a gaggle of old theatre pit musicians'), the band-bus ('a mobile dustbin'), the 'drunk, dishevelled and ranting' pop singers and their inhuman noise. It was the last quality that caused him to quit: according to the jacket, he is now reading nice quiet meters for a living.

Mahalia Jackson's deepest conviction was that her superbly powerful voice was a gift of God, and must be used only in His service: she would never sing a blues or enter a dance hall. Nevertheless, when she went north in the twenties black ministers objected to her rhythmic style (she countered with Psalm 47: 'Oh, clap your hands, all ye people'), and it was another 20 years before she sang to an integrated audience.

Her progress from Water Street, in New Orleans, to Carnegie Hall, the White House and the Vatican is interesting sociologically as well as musically: she soon turned to politics, singing for Alderman Wm. L. Dawson in the Chicago wards ('Dawson has brought us all the way, and carries our burdens'); then it was Roosevelt, and after the war Martin Luther King and the Kennedys. In the Bahamas she told her audience that the land was theirs to run.

Ms Goreau's interminable 592 pages have somewhere within them a fascinating Elmer Gantry-style book. Mahalia travelled with a circus of pianists, gospel-singers, and general hangers-on, and her two marriages foundered on this rock as much as anything. She was a tremendously hard worker and a tough business-woman: there is an amusing juxtaposition of a Japanese music critic's notice ('Though I am not a Christian, I could not help running tears') with Mahalia yelling 'You get my money, or I'll make Hell a present of you in a basket!' waving the pen-knife with which she had been cutting her corns.

In early middle age she became a permanent semi-invalid: her dreams of a Mahalia Jackson Foundation dwindled to the Mahalia Jackson Chicken Systems. But her faith never wavered: after a specially successful perform-ance, with everyone crying, an admirer asked 'How do you do it?' Mahalia fixed the full force of her being on him. 'Don't you *know*?' she said in disgust.

Guardian, 25 November 1976

43

A Jazzman's Frenzied Fragments

THE McJAZZ MANUSCRIPTS: A COLLECTION OF THE WRITINGS OF SANDY BROWN edited by David Binns (Faber, £6.95)

STEVE RACE: MUSICIAN AT LARGE (Eyre Methuen, £6.50)

The authors of both these books suffered serious illnesses in their mid-forties. Steve Race happily recovered from his heart attack and is still with us. Sandy Brown ('If I were you, Mr Brown, I would consult your own doctor as soon as you can—this afternoon if possible') died of malignant hypertension within two years of this warning.

In a way this summarises their respective characters. Sandy Brown did not take his doctor's advice and slow down: he went on playing jazz clarinet, working as an acoustic consultant, and generally having a ball. His master was veteran Johnny Dodds, who died in 1940 after making two records that everyone except Sandy Brown thought were his worst: he thought they were his best, 'out of tune, accompanied by the failing trumpet of Natty Dominique and squeaking like a loose board'.

The McJazz Manuscripts is less a book than an act of homage compiled by his erstwhile professional partner. It contains six chapters of autobiography (written by a fictitious alter ego, Alastair Habb), fifteen jazz pieces reprinted from *The Listener* (Karl Miller was an old school chum), a variety of letters mostly in a vein of private waggery but including a ferocious attack on Sir Michael Swann, Chairman of the BBC, on the decline in live jazz broadcasting, plus a discography by Alun Morgan.

To old acquaintances it is no doubt Sandy in his habit as he lived. To everyone else it cannot help being a collection of somewhat frenzied fragments that don't add up to a coherent picture: this is a pity, for Sandy Brown was clearly a remarkable man with a knowledge of jazz that was both wide and deep, as well as being able to do it.

Steve Race, on the other hand, did slow down ('just a little'), but *Musician at Large* is by comparison autobiography at its most formal: childhood, schooldays, war service, marriage, small jobs, big jobs, Frank Sinatra, Duke Ellington, Paul Robeson. A natural musician, he was led by his versatility from the Royal College of Music to playing the piano with dance bands and later in jazz clubs.

He composed, orchestrated, and accompanied both the obscure ('When I say "I'm on my way to the asylum accompanied by the orchestra" you play a chord in G') and the famous (Cleo Laine, with no notice, at the Prague International Jazz Festival). But gradually an equal conversational adroitness took over: he became increasingly on call for radio interviews, *Any Questions, PM* and finally *My Music*, developing the amiable personality that is now so well known.

Only the urbanity of his style saves the reader from a perpetually dropped jaw at Mr Race's astonishing capability: there seems nothing he cannot do, or at least have a creditable stab at. Perhaps the urbanity is laid on over thickly at times: the procession of show-biz characters, each duly complimented ('Eleanor Summerfield, a mite scatty but enchantingly full of life . . . the elegant Leonard Sachs . . . David Nixon and Tim Rice, both of them charming men with towering intellects . . . Everyone likes Roy Plomley . . . ') produces a sugar-coated effect. But Mr Race can be sharp at times: oddly enough it is the jazzmen Parker and Roland Kirk he finds unsympathetic.

But in fact jazz itself does not stay the course either, dropping out in 1963 ('it was a surfeit of live performances in clubs and concerts which was to blame'), and while no one could disagree about the drum solos (and the bass solos) Mr Race's inimitable spread of talents somehow lacks a unifying enthusiasm once it goes. It would have been nice if just one of his shows could have presented jazz as he liked it to be.

Guardian, 2 August 1979

44
Top Band Talk

THE WORLD OF COUNT BASIE by Stanley Dance (Sidgwick & Jackson, £8.95)

With Ellington gone, Basie's is top band, its ancestry reaching back to the early thirties to be lost in the Bennie Moten orchestra and Walter Page's Blue Devils. It is jazz history, and history deserves to be written.

Unfortunately, the Dance technique of hanging a microphone round the necks of thirty-odd Basieites and stringing the transcribed results together does not really make a book. For one thing, the interviews span over fifteen years, and one never gets the feel of the band at any one time. For another, what the cats like talking about is not Basie, nor his band, but themselves.[76]

This is really where the book's strength lies, lazy deltas of reminiscence winding back to before the war, before the Depression, into the Twenties and the farm childhoods ('I had a paper route, on a horse'). Most of them were born in the mid-West, and learned jazz from, and even played with, the famous territory bands such as Alphonso Trent and George E. Lee, Nat Towles and Troy Floyd; they recall half-legendary figures like drummer A. G. Godley ('the Gene Krupa of the day before yesterday') and Raymond 'Sid' Valentine, who matched Armstrong at the Savoy in 1930.

Since Basie's was a Kansas City band, some remember the youthful Parker with Jay McShann ('His tone was different, and he knew what he was doing. When he got to New York he got on this bop kick'). But they are just as likely to remember Ben Webster sassing Joe Louis in Sugar Ray's bar uptown, and what happened.

It seems to have been rather an *old* band, as jazz orchestras go: in 1947, Preston Love was the youngest member at 25, and time and again the fear of being out-dated clouds the narrative, whether by bop, or rock ('The group knew three chords, but not very well'), or simply by slowing down ('I'd like to be sitting in with one of those good studio bands in Hollywood'). This even affects Count himself ('Basie used to please people with his piano, but he got away from it when bop came along. He got shy'[77]), who emerges as a kersey uncomplicated character ('He'd have patches on his pants and everything. All his band was like that').

When Basie lost his great pre–1950 soloists, he turned increasingly to ensemble numbers, but this kind of policy switch arouses no great emotion. Gene Ramey is acute on the coming of amplification: 'All of a sudden, around '47 or '48, they started making the bass dominant and noisy with all those amplifications. It was wrong,' and specially wrong for a band with such an integrated rhythm section as Basie's.

But all in all, their time with the band was just another job, memorable maybe but easily submerged in other, richer recollections. It is trumpeter Joe Newman who produces the most devastating summing-up: 'The only reason I see why Basie's band is as well received as it is is because there aren't many other big bands.' Tell that to the crowds at the Woodside, in 1938.

Guardian, 27 November 1980

45

Crows and Daws

NIGHT CREATURE: A JOURNAL OF JAZZ, 1975–80 by Whitney Balliett
(Oxford University Press, $15.95)

Whitney Balliett's unassailable reputation as a jazz writer has a curious relation to the subculture of the jazz photograph, a genre brought into being by the insatiable appetite of jazz lovers for seeing its practitioners in the act of creation, as if their faces, momentarily frozen in distortion or distension, were part of, or even a key to, the music itself. He is not, in the accepted sense, a biographer or a historian: he has not written the definitive life of a performer or charted the musical development of a period or place. He is not a musicologist, linking by transcription free form and field-holler. What he does, primarily, is go to concerts in the music's acknowledged capital (now, as for the last fifty years, New York) and describe what he hears (in, appropriately enough, *The New Yorker*). He writes in the first-nighter tradition of Kenneth Tynan[78] and A. J. Liebling,[79] in which what is said arises from a particular occasion and is designed in part to eternalize it:

> Erroll Garner last appeared in New York at the Maisonette Room of the St. Regis in May of 1974. His playing was effulgent, and he looked as he always had—a short, gleaming, funny, cooking man, his black hair a mirror, his great parrot nose pointed into the winds of his invention. He rocked and grunted and hummed at the keyboard, and his astonishing hands—he could span thirteen notes—went like jackhammers.

Such a passage is no isolated contrivance. Balliett's writing is instinctively pictorial: simile and metaphor, adjective and adverb all cohere and jump to tell us *what it was like to be there*. The playing of Johnny Hodges ('a mysterious, shrewd, monosyllabic man, short and oval') 'gave the impression that he was lobbing the melody back and forth from hand to hand.' Wild Bill Davison 'puts his cornet just to the left of the center of his lips, aims it at third base, and beetles his brows.' 'It's a compliment to jazz,' as the first sentence of his first book ran, back in 1959, 'that nine-tenths of the voluminous writing about it is so bad'; nevertheless, it is not a compliment Balliett himself is inclined to pay:

Ellington in the flesh—his umbrous, polished voice; his gracious laugh; his accent, which was universal and aristocratic; his long, handsome, beautifully lived-in face; his careful, philosopher's gait; his locked concentration when he worked . . .

And his attention fastens as readily on the music itself, sometimes with hit-or-miss impressionism:

Gillespie liked to clown and blare and do the fandango up and down his registers. He liked to blow the grass flat and divide the waters.

At other times Balliett writes in dissecting slow motion:

He would start a solo with half a dozen low, breathy staccato notes jammed together, repeat them and pause, rise almost an octave to a flickering, half-sounded note, and, before this ascension had registered on the ear, drop back to a more staccato breathiness and into a dodging, undulating stretch of notes that had a Giacometti sound.

Whether this kind of paragraph (and there is a good deal more of it) really tells a listener who has never heard him what Pee Wee Russell sounds like is a matter for conjecture, but Balliett uses the technique constantly. By now he has worked through most of the main drummers (seemingly his first love) and has begun on the pianists.

But every so often he unites these talents in a larger tapestry. He will visit a player, tape what he says, and carefully interweave large stretches of this vernacular with his own studied narrative, achieving what in the trade is called a profile but is really a Van Dyck portrait. Two such pieces in an earlier collection—on Russell and Henry 'Red' Allen—are triumphs of this method, making up a lovingly detailed diptych. Balliett admired both players (he brought them together to make records more than once), seeing them both as imprisoned in limiting and ultimately alien traditions, and his vignettes of their different ways of living are done with a novelist's precision. One cannot recall the scruffy, transient Russell apartment and the meal at the neighbouring eating house without remembering the contrast of Allen, the family man, checking his granddaughters' homework before sitting down to a dish of fried chicken and cabbage with his guest. After reading such pieces, one has somehow met these men, heard them play, and read their full-scale biographies—and ever after these impressions will dominate one's idea of them. The achievement is the more remarkable by reason of the gentle courtesy with which it is done.

The fascination of a Balliett collection lies in watching his hypersensitive technique (a combination of Leica and lapel mike) receive and transmit so many various musical experiences. For various they are: a performance of Joplin's rare *Treemonisha*, Ray Charles and Cleo Laine doing *Porgy and Bess*, Scott Hamilton, Benny Goodman, Anthony Braxton, Adolphus Cheatham—each one handled with the same vivid perception as if to demonstrate that somewhere among them lies a common denominator. In his first book, Balliett called the fifties 'the most bewildering years in the music's brief history,' but they can hardly have been as bewildering as the period recorded here. Reading *Night Creature* is like picking one's way through what seems alternately a battlefield, an archaeological site, and a deserted museum. What was in the fifties still barely discernible as one music is now a shredded and fractured continuum in which ninety-nine-year-old Eubie Blake ('whose fingers stroke up and down the keyboard like trireme oars') finds himself on the same bill as Ornette Coleman and Cecil Taylor. What was happy entertainment is now harsh didacticism, when it is not part of a glum college syllabus.

Such a situation would seem beyond the compass of a single human sensibility, yet somehow Balliett manages to contain it. Consider his extended account (May 1922, 1977) of the Association for the Advancement of Creative Musicians (one of whose mottoes is 'We are opposed to the word jazz. Jazz means nigger music'). This series of grant-supported concerts ('the total attendance was probably about four hundred') was clearly an excruciating experience of pure duration:

> The AACM has a galactic sense of time. Its concerts begin forty to fifty minutes late, and intermissions last half an hour. The musicians wander on and off the stage in slow motion. Their solos are often Coltranean in length, and their numbers—in order not to mistakenly lock out a soloist before he is done—sometimes last a couple of hours.

Yet Balliett—who on another page says of early jazz, 'This lovely polyphonic music thrived at least twenty-five years'—stays on his feet till the final bell, contriving to suggest that he has even enjoyed some of it. He sees the Association as having 'a determination to bring into being a new and durable music—a hard-nosed utopian music, without racial stigmata, without clichés, and without commercialism,' and treats its practitioners with the same elegant exactitude as he does Bix Beiderbecke and Lester Young:

> No sooner has he completed one virtuoso bit of business than he is off on the next. These included four consecutive—almost overlapping—ascending arpeggios played in sixty-fourth notes and in different keys; a muted passage in which he seems to play two melodic lines at once; an open-horn passage in which, after having sprayed water into his mouthpiece, he sounded like an echo chamber [et cetera].

No doubt this was all very striking. But, as Eddie 'Lockjaw' Davis said in 1970, 'Who is going to pay a second time to hear a guy wearing a sheet go rootle-tootle up and down the scale?'

Balliett, in short, recalls Arnold Bennett's impatient comment, 'Hang Eddie Marsh! He's a miserable fellow—he enjoys everything.'[80] And indeed there comes a point when Balliett's role as pure sensibility, proposing nothing and imposing nothing, starts to drag a little. None of the complimentary remarks about Balliett and his other books reproduced on the jacket of this one uses the word 'critic,' and this may well be significant. For a critic, after all, is a man who likes some things and dislikes others, and finds reasons for doing so and for trying to persuade other people to do so. This is altogether alien to Balliett's purpose.[81] He wishes, or so it seems, to transmit, to reproduce, and so to preserve, knowing that anyone who writes down what he sees and hears for twenty-five years will in spite of himself become a historian of a different, and perhaps rarer, quality than the term usually implies. This is what he has done, and is presumably what he wanted to do.

Not, of course, that he is in any way incapable of criticism. There is a capsule history of jazz on page 200, over almost before it has started, that ends, 'But what a lonely and illusory music!' It is a sudden and plangent passage, awakening in the reader a desire for a quite different Balliett book; but the next moment we are at Hopper's listening to Jim Hall and Bob Brookmeyer. Nor are his evocations free from hostility. An extended account of a Keith Jarrett concert left at least one reader convinced, without having heard him, that he is no good. Since Balliett is a master of language, this must be the impression he means to convey, but he nowhere comes within a mile of saying it. He looses off both barrels on successive nights at Sarah Vaughan ('no more intelligible than moos') and Betty Carter ('she is hard going'), but the condemnation is so carefully argued, and with so many qualifications, that it almost sounds like a compliment.

Any writer in Balliett's position is committed to the continuous present; it is hard for him to step back and say what it all adds up to. Even when, in his more extended pieces, he takes a holiday from it, however, he leans heavily on the technique of the recorded interview (there are two illuminating encounters in *Night Creature* with Jimmy McPartland and Nellie Lutcher—who would have thought she played with Bunk Johnson?), and despite the unfaultable historical knowledge that underpins everything he writes, there is still a lack of final assessment not forced on him by the occasional nature of his engagement. Compared with a theater critic such as James Agate, who wrote a weekly column in the *Sunday Times* for about thirty years, Balliett has no critical position. Agate's was clear: 'Ne'er look, ne'er look; the eagles are gone: crows and daws, crows and daws!' No one, in short, was likely to equal Irving, Bernhardt, and the rest of the titans of his youth. It was a sweeping principle, but it meant that Agate's praise was worth having. With Balliett one is not so sure. Can the answer be that as long as any jazz player is being filtered through the transcendence of Balliett's prose and perception, he is as good as any of his predecessors? It is a paradoxical situation.[82] Perhaps Balliett should have a talk with Lockjaw Davis.

American Scholar, 51 (1981–2)

46

Wandering Minstrels

DIZZY: THE AUTOBIOGRAPHY OF DIZZY GILLESPIE with Al Fraser (Allen, £9.95)

JAZZ AWAY FROM HOME by Chris Goddard (Paddington Press, £7.50)

It is hard to realise that Dizzy Gillespie is now an elder statesman of jazz, older than King Oliver, guest of successive U.S. Presidents, a spokesman for his people, and no longer the clowning bop revolutionary, the 'other heartbeat' of Charlie Parker who died a quarter of a century ago.

This monumental account (at 552 pages it must be the longest book about any single jazzman) unfolds how it happens. Although musically Parker and Gillespie were 'like one guy with two heads', as Ray Brown puts it, they were completely different characters. Despite his soubriquet, Gillespie was businesslike, ambitious, unsquashable ('Dizzy is a very strong person,' says Max Roach): he could not stand Parker's unpunctuality and drug addiction, and the two men parted. Brilliant and dependable, Gillespie went on to lead a big band (*Metronome*'s Band of the Year, 1947), to play Carnegie Hall, to tour, to teach.

The book is a tessellation of taped voices: Dizzy of course tells his own story, but there are numerous interjections, mostly from the scores of musicians who played with him, sometimes describing incidents from different viewpoints. Much of it is fascinating, some of it boring: more editing would have helped. Gillespie's dedication to his own virtuosity comes out strongly, as does his insouciant spirit ('I've never really wanted to be a millionaire: I just want to live like one') and the support of his formidable wife Lorraine. Despite his balanced acceptance of other jazz modes ('I didn't dig Ornette at the beginning') and his present eminence, it is hard not to feel that he never quite survived the bop era that he helped create.[83]

Jazz Away From Home is a detailed account of the arrival of jazz in Europe after 1918 and its acceptance there up to the Depression. Here too are interviews: Arthur Briggs, Bill Dillard, 'Bricktop', Ray Ventura and many more, together with contemporary newspaper reports, music criticism and photographs. What the American Negro liked about France was the absence of racial discrimination: what France liked about jazz is less clear. Partly it was show business, partly the 'latest craze', partly a musical curiosity that hooked Milhaud and Ravel. There are extraordinary glimpses, such as Dave Tough and Scott Fitzgerald making up limericks together. The cut-off point, though arguable, seems arbitrary: perhaps it is just that one wants more of a thoroughly fascinating exposition.

Unpublished

This piece seems to have been commissioned by the Guardian. *The PLPBJL archive preserves Larkin's typescript and an accompanying slip from the paper's Literary Editor; the latter is dated 18 February, with no year given. However, the PLPBJL catalogue cites 18 February 1983 as date of composition: this is most unlikely, since the Gillespie autobiography was published in the spring of 1980. In any event, the review was never published, either in the* Guardian *or anywhere else.*

47

Pleasing the People

LOUIS ARMSTRONG by James Lincoln Collier (Michael Joseph, £12.95)

It is tempting to say that one could do without any twentieth-century artist sooner than Louis Armstrong,[84] for while the rest were pulling their media to pieces, Armstrong was giving jazz its first definitive voice, one that has changed the character of popular music down to the present day. His life became an allegory of genius transcending the accidents of poverty and race; simple and modest in his personality, imperially authoritative in his work, he had by the end of his life grown into an internationally-accepted symbol not only of jazz but of good will and good humour.

James Lincoln Collier does not dissent from this view, but he dissects it, and this gives his book an inner disharmony as well as a few nasty jolts to received opinion. Armstrong was not born on 4 July, for instance, nor in 1900; he knocked two years off his age when registering for the draft in 1918. He was not named Daniel. But these are minor matters. Tradition has it that after the first amazing exuberance of the Twenties Armstrong progressively refined his style until at the end of his life a simple enunciation of the melody embodied jazz more purely than the wildest improvisation.

Collier does not deny the exuberance: he is a Hot Five man, one for whom the recordings made in Chicago between 1925 and 1928 display a richness and technical virtuosity Armstrong was rarely to equal, and a chapter is devoted to analysing their importance. But the refinement is something else. Collier claims it was the result of lip damage caused by a faulty embouchure; by 1929, 'his lip was in ruins.' He simply could not sustain his early brilliance.

In a key chapter 'The Fork in the Road' Collier asks why, with the Hot Five records behind him ('one of the most significant bodies of American recorded music'), Armstrong chose a career of stage mugging, eye-rolling vocals and high C's. Why was such a prodigious talent so prodigally wasted? First, Armstrong was born into the black working class, and never escaped its limitations. Slavery was only two generations away; to be an entertainer was one of the few ways out of the grinding insecurity of day-labour, and then only with a white man's hand on his shoulder ('This is my nigger'). And entertainment was not art, or self-expression: it was 'pleasing the people,' as in the minstrel tent. This accounts for his repertoire of coon songs, ballads and flagwavers, and his subservience to a succession of ruthless managers who treated him simply as a performing animal. Even Joe Glaser, who gave Armstrong's life the stability it needed after the mid-Thirties, 'collected the money, paid the bills, and gave Armstrong whatever he decided Armstrong ought to have,' at the same time driving him mercilessly.

Secondly, Armstrong was by temperament shy, indecisive and easily put down. He liked to have his mind made up for him. His second wife, Lil Hardin, made him leave Oliver for Henderson, and Henderson for cabarets and theatre work: she was right both times. (Lil's life after Armstrong left her is touching: she stayed in the house they had shared, surrounded by relics of him: she died while playing at his memorial concert in 1971.) His managers picked his bandsmen. He did not like competition; the story of his flight to France when Jack Hylton booked Coleman Hawkins to play alongside him is well known. He was jealous of his fellow-musicians; Pops Foster, while admitting that you had to be good to play with Armstrong, said that if you were too good you were out.

All this produced a slavish thirst for applause. He couldn't get enough of it: every night a fresh audience, a fresh acclamation, fully compensated for the exhausting routine of travelling. 'That's what I want, the audience,' he said. 'I want to hear that applause.' His work became stereotyped rather than refined: 'On the first chorus I plays the melody, on the second chorus I plays the melody around the melody, and on the third chorus I routines.' 'Routining' meant simple repetition, clichés, High C's, nothing calling for any agility of lip. By the time of the All Stars, Armstrong had long since given up jazz in favour of crowd-pleasing and resting his chops. Only in the recording studio did he sometimes return to the art of which he was truly a master, and then only at the insistence of the record companies.

This is all profoundly depressing, the depressingness of the half-truth. What does Collier expect Armstrong to have done about it? Turn himself into Miles Davis? Put the Negro question forward 50 years?[85] And the half-truthfulness keeps Collier dashing backwards and forwards between contrasting viewpoints. Armstrong was over the hill by 1933, but there were those wonderful Hot Five remakes in 1957. When Armstrong found he could sing, 'the loss to jazz was incalculable,' but he 'was one of the great singers of popular songs of his time.' In *Ain't Misbehavin* 'the signs of his artistic exhaustion . . . are already present. And yet the record is fundamentally a strong performance.' And so on.

For that matter, can any depressing book about Armstrong be more than half true? What is lacking is Armstrong himself, that chuckling verbatim vernacular, talking or writing, that Jones and Chilton[86] used so effectively in their 1971 biography and which was so immediately convincing:

> Ain't no such thing as getting tired of playing a number. Paul Robeson, when he got up to sing *Old Man River*, may have been a million times, but he sung it good . . . You'll always get critics of showmanship. Critics in England say I was a clown, but a clown, that's hard. If you can make people chuckle a little; it's happiness to me to see people happy, and most of the people who criticise don't know one note from another.

This may be just what Collier has been saying, but in Louis's words it is brightening, as if Louis himself had suddenly come into the room, bringing with him all the beauty and excitement and high spirits that he dispensed so effortlessly, and demonstrating that he was something more than an end-product of compulsions and compromises—a great artist, a great personality, a great human being. The nearest Collier comes to this is when he quotes Danny Baker's description of Armstrong in his crowded dressing-room:

> He be sittin' in his underwear with a towel round his lap, one round his shoulders an' that white handkerchief on his head, and he'd put that grease around his lips. Look like a minstrel man, ya know . . . an' laughin' you know natural the way he is . . . Got their eyes dead on him, just like they was lookin' at a diamond.

Observer, 25 March 1984

48
Home Cooking

A HISTORY OF JAZZ IN BRITAIN 1919–50 by Jim Godbolt (Quartet, £14.95)

Very much a buy for Old Nostalgians, this evocation of the England of George V, *Nash's Magazine* and the Children's Hour, with Ambrose at the Embassy and Harry Roy at the Mayfair, and the struggles of the new subversion, jazz, to be heard, understood and accepted. Simply the mention of *Rhythm* with its ten Hove cartoon covers, the scarlet, black and gold Vocalion labels, and Leonard Hibbs's 'Twenty One Years of Swing Music' reawakens the vertiginous excitement of Fats Waller records from Radio Luxembourg, Billy Cotton's 'St Louis Blues' (trumpet and vocal refrain: Teddy Foster), and the curtain going up on Nat Gonella and his Georgians in their blue and white striped blazers. Bliss was it in that dawn.[87]

But Mr Godbolt's substantial book aims much higher than this. It chronicles not only the landmarks of the new music's appearance—the first visits of Louis Armstrong and Duke Ellington, HMV's First Public Jam Session—but the founding (and too often foundering) of specialist magazines, the early discographers, the Rhythm Clubs and their recitals, and the legendary locations such as the Jigs' Club and the Bag o' Nails. Mr Godbolt quotes liberally from the early jazz journals, and the narrative is piquantly supported by his own personal involvement in much of what he relates (for more of this, see his autobiography *All This and 10%*).[88]

As in America, jazz is met with horrified incomprehension (George Robey told the management of the London Hippodrome that either the

Original Dixieland Jazz Band would have to go, or he would) and moral disapproval, but the most lasting opposition seems to have come from the professional dance-band musicians of the day, or at least from their union, culminating in the Ministry of Labour's ban on foreign (i.e. American) musicians in 1935 'until satisfactory reciprocal arrangements had been made.' Godbolt has referred before to the limited pit-orchestra mentality of the Musicians' Union of the day, but the notion that the appearance of Duke Ellington at the Palladium could do English musicians out of a job, or that 'reciprocal arrangements' could exist in any real sense where one side had everything and the other nothing, was beneath even their level.

What really roused their hostility was the suspicion that this new music was going to undermine their livelihood by being popular in a way they couldn't manage, and break up the social pattern on which their existence depended. And they were right. The latterday careers of the lords of the white-tie world of the Thirties were pitiful in the extreme, huddled over metered gas fires in Brighton bed-sitters, the walls hung with signed photographs of deposed royalties. Jazz, says Mr Godbolt rather unkindly, 'sounded the death-knell of these baton-waving frock-coated mountebanks.'

The book is full of unexpected felicities, such as Mrs Thatcher playing clarinet with Chris Barber and Kenny Ball, or the story that Armstrong's anti-bop version of *The Whiffenpoof Song* was withdrawn in Britain at the request of the Kipling Society, on the grounds that it was based on 'Gentlemen-Rankers.' The fact that Mr Godbolt spells it Wiffenpoof, and calls the poem 'Gentleman Ranker,' and gets the words that Louis sings slightly wrong, provokes the criticism that references have not always been verified.

The LP of Spanier's Ragtimers was 'The Great Sixteen,' not 'The Glorious Sixteen,' so it didn't echo Edgar Jackson's laudatory adjective; the first version to be issued of Henry Allen's 'Swing Out' was the third take, not the first, though this still exemplifies Mr Godbolt's assertion that the first issue is usually the best. David Boulton's *Jazz In Britain* (1958) is not mentioned in the text or the bibliography. Most curious is the failure to reinforce the irony of Ken 'Snakehips' Johnson's declaration that he would make swing popular at the Café de Paris or die in the attempt by pointing out that Johnson, along with his tenor sax Dave Williams, was killed when the Café received a direct hit in March 1941.[89]

No mention is made of the Traditional Jazz Concert at the Festival Hall on 14 July 1950, which, attended by HRH Princess Elizabeth and productive of four excellent Parlophone 78s, could well have stood for the final 'arrival' of jazz in this country. In fact 1950 seems rather an arbitrary cut-off point. The next decade—say up to the emergence of the Beatles —saw jazz commercially successful in Britain as well as socially acceptable, and to take the story up to this consummation would have made a more satisfying book.

Mr Godbolt hints that the present volume may have a successor, which would be delightful, but it is likely to be sadder, for it will have to relate the subsidence of this unique art to a minority interest once again as the extravagances of pop music engulfed us. On reflection, even the present narrative has an undertone of melancholy. If Britain had produced a single figure of the stature of Django Reinhardt, her standing in the jazz world would be very different.[90] It is to Mr Godbolt's credit that he never pretends that his tale is other than one of belated recognition and inadequate emulation.

Observer, 12 August 1984

Part One: Notes

1 Hugues Panassié (1912–74) was a founder and then president of the Hot Club of France, and from 1935–46 editor of *Jazz hot* magazine. His work-rate was as pronounced as his enthusiasm, and his 1934 book *Le Jazz Hot* remains important for being amongst the first studies to treat jazz with due seriousness. The celebrated 'Panassié sessions' took place in 1938—a series of small group recordings with Mezzrow and *inter alia* Sidney Bechet and trumpeter Tommy Ladnier (1900–39). Reflecting on them and on Mezzrow's art in *The Real Jazz*, Panassié wrote: '[His] greatest claim to fame is the fact that he plays the blues better than any other white musician, and I am not speaking of clarinetists only—he plays the blues in the same way as the great Negro musicians. Likewise the luminous melodic intelligence of his solos, his fine sense of collective improvisation, and his intuition which equals that of Jimmie Noone, certainly reveal why Mezzrow is by far the greatest jazz clarinetist that the white race has produced.'

Remarks such as those suggest that Larkin's choice of 'gullible' was more than justified; it is unsurprising that Panassié's star waned soon afterwards. Always conservative, he was appalled by the rise of bebop, and denied it jazz status altogether. To borrow Larkin's term, he was an unbudging—even fanatical—'Gibbon' (see Note 16 below), and while the value of his contribution to jazz is assured, few would now regard him as reliable.

2 A typically adroit analogy. It might seem to do Mezzrow too much honour, but the point at issue is that both were *sui generis*.

3 William Empson (1906–84) was one of the twentieth century's most influential literary critics. The reference is to his *Some Versions of Pastoral* (1935), which identified the ideal simplicity of the pastoral convention in a far wider range of literature than had previously been essayed.

4 Edited by journalist George Scott, *Truth* was a weekly magazine which enjoyed a limited vogue in the 1950s, and has been typified by Anthony Thwaite (in a personal communication with the editors) as 'left wing Tory in sympathy'. In addition to Larkin, Bernard Levin and Katherine Whitehorn were among its regular book reviewers.

Writing to a friend in 1957, Larkin confided, 'I am contemplating refusing all further reviewing jobs, bar jazz ones for *Truth*: my poor brain finds them too much trouble.' To Robert Conquest, 26 June 1957: *Selected Letters*, 277.

5 A remarkable image, not least because it occurs so early in Larkin's jazz *oeuvre*—a full decade before the Introduction to *All What Jazz* was composed. Despite the text's implication, the paradisial associations identified are Larkin's, not Ramsey and Smith's, and the witty audacity of the parallel neither disguises nor dilutes the underlying depth of feeling: this was the jazz that Larkin loved with an undimmed passion all his life.

6 Nat Shapiro and Nat Hentoff, eds., *Hear Me Talkin' To Ya: The Story of Jazz by the Men Who Made It* (New York: Rinehart and Co. Inc., 1955), a collection of reminiscences, described by Humphrey Lyttelton as 'a fascinating book which should forthwith become every jazz fan's *vade-mecum*'.

7 Norman Granz (b. 1918), impresario. The chief reference here would appear to be to Jazz At The Philharmonic, the all-star travelling 'circus' which Granz launched at the Philharmonic Theatre in Los Angeles in 1944. The initiative was enormously successful and (therefore) controversial: many found his concerts vulgar and formulaic. No less successful or controversial were his exploits as a record producer, especially after his creation of Verve in 1956. He sold the label to MGM in 1961, but returned to jazz recording when he founded Pablo in 1972.

8 Another felicitous combination of wit and passion. Those prejudiced against jazz have always associated it with the occult, with 'jungle magic' and all that is tawdry and undesirable; those prejudiced against Larkin might therefore be anxious to see this sentence as fresh evidence of his 'racism'. As one hopes is obvious, Larkin is in fact celebrating the African-American creation of a noble and unique art form, and in the process having some not-so-gentle fun at *real* racists' expense.

9 The Institute of Jazz Studies is at Rutgers University, Newark, New Jersey. Its current Director is Dan Morgenstern.

10 This sentence could be seen as an early 'telegraphing' of Larkin's dislike of modernism in general and bop in particular, and may indeed be so. But he clearly approves of the author's intellectual rigour in making the point, and his tone suggests that at the very least Stearns has produced a case to answer.

11 Chano Pozo (1915–48), Cuban drummer, singer and dancer. And concerning 'equally significant': there is a good deal of evidence to suggest that this is a

gibe. See, for example, **[45]** and Note 80 below on the suspect nature of 'liking everything'.

12 A reference to Michael Henchard, the tragic hero of Thomas Hardy's novel *The Mayor of Casterbridge* (1886). Henchard's middle age as a successful public figure is haunted and eventually destroyed by his squalid past—primarily the selling of his wife at auction. However, Larkin's adjective is more probably prompted by Henchard's no less fundamental propensity for making bad decisions at crucial times.

13 The Cotton Club was the proverbial 'big break' for Ellington, proving decisive in launching his career. He later cited the engagement as 'a classic example of being at the right place at the right time with the right thing before the right people'. That might serve as a good definition of 'luck'; it is, equally, a good definition of genius and/or acumen. King Oliver's 'Henchardian' nature (see Note 12 above) presumably favoured the former definition.

14 Reviewed by Larkin for *Truth*, 26 July 1957; see **[2]**.

15 American jazz magazine. Founded in 1884, *Metronome* covered the music scene in general until 1935, when George T. Simon took over as editor; thereafter, until it ceased publication in 1961, it devoted itself entirely to jazz. Although never rivalling *Down Beat* in influence or sustained readership, *Metronome* enjoyed considerable popularity in the 1940s and 1950s, partly because of its annual polls to determine readers' favourite instrumentalists and bands and its further initiative in assembling such poll-winners for recording sessions. This practice came to an end in 1956.

Larkin's review of George T. Simon's book on the big band era can be found on pages 82–3 above **[36]**.

16 Larkin's distinction between 'Wells and Gibbon' historians of jazz is one he made a number of times; the *locus classicus* is the *Daily Telegraph* column of 15 August 1970, reprinted in both *All What Jazz* and *Required Writing*. The paper chose 'Onwards and Downwards' as the piece's title; for its future incarnations Larkin replaced that with 'Wells or Gibbon?' The review finds Larkin at his most acute, at once imaginative and resolved; its conclusion is definitive.

> Behind this confrontation, I fancy, lies a number of opposed prejudices. The Wellses want to extend terms, to stretch points, to see things change. The Gibbons want words to keep their meanings, to be definite, to see things stay the same . . . Duke [Ellington] is a Wells; Louis Armstrong . . . is a Gibbon.
>
> Well, either camp has a pretty good leader. All I would say to my critics is that the jazz that conquered the world (and me) . . . is dying with its practitioners, Red Allen, Pee Wee Russell, Johnny Hodges. Not to admit this is—well, holding back history.

Larkin may count himself a Gibbon—he obviously does—but his awareness of the Wellses' appeal is a good deal more sensitive than many have acknowledged. His appraisal of Ulanov's case in the review at issue bears that out further.

17 Amis's Foreword includes the observation that 'At a time when jazz musicians are flocking into the conservatoire, setting themselves up as little Honeggers and Milhauds, maundering about "tone-masses" and "aesthetic principles of unity", literally and figuratively turning their backs on the audience, one welcomes an assertion of the primary and peculiar qualities of the music.' He also endorsed Ulanov's assertion that for 'modern' jazz artists 'no condemnation seems so terrible as that of being "dated" '. Larkin—whose tastes in jazz were similar to Amis's—would have taken particular satisfaction from his final comment that perhaps 'when we can write "irresponsible" for "dated" . . . jazz will have come of age'.

18 Larkin's use here of the verb *deals with* presents an interesting minor puzzle: is it intended denotatively (in the sense of 'covered') or connotatively—i.e. 'put properly in his place'? By this time (1958) Brubeck was a controversial figure: his quartet (with alto saxophonist Paul Desmond, drummer Joe Morello and bassist Eugene Wright, who had recently replaced Norman Bates) was extremely popular on the college circuit and rapidly growing in general appeal. He would soon have a top-ten hit with Desmond's composition 'Take Five', which confirmed any critics in their view of his music as gimmicky and unacceptably populist; Brubeck's own piano playing was particularly vilified.

Contemporaneous references in *All What Jazz* are hardly friendly, but neither do they suggest outright hostility. *Take Five* is judged as 'a modest tricky-rhythmed piece' that 'seems an odd candidate for mass acclaim' (November 1961); three months later he describes Brubeck's then-latest album **Time Further Out** as an

> LP of new tempo-rarities . . . in which the Quartet waltz and otherwise gyrate through nine time-signatures ranging from 3/4 to 9/8 . . . and (Brubeck's) new titles, especially *Blue Shadows In The Street*, are pleasantly fascinating.

However, that mild encomium is then torpedoed:

> But they reminded me of John Hammond's comment on Benny Carter's *Waltzing The Blues:* 'In monkeying with the structure of the blues, Benny has robbed them of all warmth and feeling.' This was in 1936, but I have never forgotten it.

Further: in July 1964, while admitting that Brubeck's records 'may be relied upon to contain a few of those moments when the proceedings drift away on a long ripple of understanding between him and Paul Desmond that evokes an answering wave of applause', he finds the pianist guilty of 'rhythmic deadness' and the music as a whole characterised by 'a battery of unvarying devices', That said, it is worth noting that when Brubeck eschewed those 'tempo-rarities' and cut an 'ordinary' album (**Angel Eyes**, reviewed in November

1965), Larkin welcomed it as evidence of a 'talent refreshed', praising its 'forthright enthusiasm' in general and Brubeck's 'unaffected swinginess' in particular.

Overall, therefore, it is reasonable to infer from *deals with* a fair degree of impatience at Brubeck's pretentiousness and often-clumping pianism, but not absolute censure. And given Larkin's views on jazz as a once-universal folk art that eventually turned its back on the audience (see particularly the *Weekend Telegraph* piece of 23 April 1965), Brubeck's early–60s popularity may have occasioned a certain ambivalence in him.

19 Larkin's pleasure in this anecdote reminds one of his musicality as a poet. Trevor Tolley has noted Larkin's observation in his workbooks: 'Writing poetry is playing off the natural rhythms and word-order of speech against the artificialities of rhyme and metre.' (Quoted in Tolley's address to the Philip Larkin Society, 'What The Notebooks Show Us—And What They Don't', 1 July 1998.) *Mutatis mutandis*, that remark also furnishes a definition of the jazz art.

20 In the jazz argot of the 1950s, a 'mouldie figge' was a hidebound reactionary who rejected all alleged 'jazz' beyond a certain date or stage of evolution as inauthentic and decadent—precisely the *persona* that Larkin often assumed.

21 F. R. Leavis (1905–78) was arguably the most influential literary critic of his generation. He was responsible, in George Steiner's words, for 're-shaping the inner landscape of taste,' resurrecting the reputations of several major writers—Conrad, Hopkins and above all Lawrence—while simultaneously offering thunderously dismissive revaluations of many others.

Sir John Squire (1884–1958) was centrally identified with the Georgian movement and the 'old' literary establishment. He attracted enormous animosity for his scathing rejection of the 'new', which he saw as dangerous literary bolshevism. Contemptuous of T. S. Eliot, he was especially belligerent about the war poetry of Owen and his ilk. John Gross provides a suitably acidic summary:

> [Squire] and his friends were associated with everything that an intellectual of the day was likely to wince at most—cricketing week-ends, foaming tankards, Sussex-by-the-sea, pale green pastorals, thigh-slapping joviality. It only needed someone to have the bright idea of christening them the Squirearchy, and the legend was complete.
>
> [*The Rise And Fall of the Man of Letters*, Pelican, 1973, 262]

Larkin's parallel is characteristically acute; what emerges from this review in particular and the collection as a whole is his conviction that both the Leavises and the Squires—whether in literature or in jazz—are equally flawed in their polarised ways.

22 A reference to the 'lily-white' Frisco Jazz Band, led by trumpeter Bob Scobey, which sought to revive the virtues of traditional jazz, especially the emphasis

on the whole band rather than on the role of the individual soloists. Other key figures in this outfit were trumpeters Lu Watters and Turk Murphy (mentioned in this piece) and pianist Ralph Sutton.

23 Much the same point was made many years later by Bernard Levin in 'Odd, The American Sound of Music' (*The Times*, 5 February 1981, 14). However, although his essay includes warmly cogent appraisals of Cole Porter, George Gershwin, Jerome Kern and other leading exponents of the American Song, it ignores jazz completely. This would suggest that the 'clear sight' for which Larkin praises Newton is still a minority facility: myopia remains the norm.

24 A slightly sardonic reference to the series of **Songbooks**, showcasing the work of America's songwriters, which Ella Fitzgerald recorded during the 1950s under the supervision of Norman Granz.

25 Sociologist Emory S. Bogardus applied the concept of 'social distance' to race relations. White Americans, he suggested, have been willing to associate—in varying degrees—with members of some forty ethnic groups, based on perceptions of skin colour. African-Americans, Hindus, Japanese, and Koreans were at the bottom of the list; the English, Canadians and Scots were at the top. See Emory S. Bogardus, 'Comparing Racial Distance in Ethiopia, South Africa, and the United States', *Sociology and Social Research*, 52 (1968), 149–56. Again, the encyclopaedic range of Larkin's knowledge is no less notable for being implied rather than paraded.

26 An important remark. In the space of a decade (1960–68) Larkin reviewed four of Oliver's books, but while the tone is invariably respectful, it is never fully enthusiastic, and this concluding demur suggests why. One senses that amidst his admiration for the work of a scholar of international distinction, Larkin wishes that Oliver could *enjoy* blues music rather more than he appears to. The pleasure principle is as central to Larkin's critical stance as to his response as listener and indeed to his work as a poet.

27 See Note 1 above.

28 (Sir) (John Frederick) Neville Cardus (1889–1975), music critic and essayist, was equally renowned as a writer on cricket, and it is in that latter capacity, of course, that he is cited here. The reference is peculiarly apposite, and not just because of Larkin's love of the game (though he never wrote about it) and his commensurate passion for music, albeit of a different *genre*.

29 A. J. Liebling (1904–1963): American journalist, war correspondent and satirist. In *The Sweet Science* (1956), he offered a series of sketches on boxers and boxing (which amongst all else had a decisive influence on the work of his then associate, Norman Mailer). Like Balliett, Liebling worked regularly for the *New Yorker*.

30 This is less approvingly tolerant than it might appear. See Introduction.

31 Orrin Keepnews and Bill Grauer Jr., *A Pictorial History of Jazz: People and Places from New Orleans to Modern Jazz* (New York, 1956; revised editions 1966 and

1981). Initially a journalist and author, Keepnews became chiefly famous for his work as a record producer. In the mid–1950s he founded and ran Riverside Records, sponsoring seminal recordings by pianists Thelonious Monk and Bill Evans and the still-contentious *Freedom Suite* by Sonny Rollins. In 1966 Keepnews founded Milestone records, and although he was eventually bought out by Fantasy, Inc., he remained active as a producer for the label.

32 Pete Lala's was a New Orleans jazz club, 1300 Customhouse Street, at Marais Street. Named after its owner (real name Pete Ciaccio), it flourished from 1906 to 1917, operating a non-segregationist policy.

Birdland, amongst the most legendary of New York's jazz clubs, took its name from Charlie Parker's soubriquet, opening on 15 December 1949 with Parker playing. It became Count Basie's New York headquarters during the 50s, and thanks to its investment in radio- and recording-technology it became additionally famous for in-person recordings, by *inter alia* John Coltrane and Basie himself.

Like so many jazz clubs, Birdland's fortunes dwindled rapidly in the late 1960s, and it was eventually taken over by the rock 'n' roll singer Lloyd Price. But its importance as a jazz venue continues to be celebrated, not least via Weather Report's huge 1976 hit 'Birdland', written by Joe Zawinul and later supplied with lyrics by Manhattan Transfer.

33 Frank Teschemacher, clarinettist. He was heavily influenced by Bix Beiderbecke, favouring the cornetist's predilection for accented ninths and elevenths; even so, one is tempted to find 'Panassié's friend' either aurally challenged or entirely ignorant of jazz musicians' skill (possibly both).

34 'Django' was written by the MJQ's pianist and leader John Lewis and was first recorded in December 1954. Impeccably structured and darkly sonorous, it bears no obvious musical relation to its eponymous inspiration, although the guitarist would surely have enjoyed its more extrovert sections.

35 The elegant wit of Larkin's censure here only thinly disguises his rage at such partiality—and rage on two counts. One is the sheer amateurishness of Brunn's historicism: Larkin understates the case with his sequent sentence, 'This utter lack of context is damaging.' The other is wholesome disgust at Brunn's calculated racism.

36 Larkin certainly did 'say a good deal on this point' elsewhere. It underscores not only the Introduction to *All What Jazz* (where Green's remark is re-quoted and elaborated upon in full measure) but, implicitly and explicitly, many of the other pieces collected here. However, Larkin's views on the development from diatonic to chromatic-based jazz amount to something much more complex than mere rejection.

37 The praise for Green's survey may itself be 'reluctant,' but Larkin understands how inevitable were the developments of the recent past, even if he is thereby full of foreboding about the future.

38 Larkin gives no provenance for this 'quotation', but it strongly recalls an episode in Huckleberry Finn, Chapter 32 (Penguin edition, 291). In recent years, Twain's masterpiece has been (ludicrously) condemned as 'racist' by some politically correct American critics; one suspects that Larkin would have enjoyed the irony and identified with it.

> 'It warn't the grounding. That didn't keep us back but a little. We blowed out a cylinder head.'
> 'Good gracious! Anybody hurt?'
> 'No'm. Killed a nigger.'
> 'Well, it's lucky, because sometimes people do get hurt . . . '

39 No provenance is offered here either, but it is absolutely of a piece with these remarks by Dvořák published in the *New York Herald*, 21 May 1893:

> I am now satisfied that the future music of this country must be founded on what are called the negro melodies. This must be the real foundation of any serious and original school of composition to be developed in the United States.

40 Sir Thomas Gresham (1519?–79), English financier and merchant. 'Gresham's Law' was the name given to the economic maxim that if a debased or depreciated currency circulates with money of high value in terms of precious metals, the 'bad money drives out the good' because of hoarding. Intriguingly, the 'inversion' of that law not only characterises the era Larkin is concerned with here but also the early 1960s.

41 The populist trad-boom in England in the early 1960s led many to investigate other 'real stuff' jazz; the same can be said for tenor saxophonist Stan Getz's success with 'Desafinado' and **Jazz Samba** in 1962, 'The Girl From Ipanema' and **Getz/Gilberto** just over a year later, and the aforementioned following enjoyed by Dave Brubeck, especially after 'Take Five' in 1961 (see Note 18 above). Conversely, the anathema (in terms of mass or even 'ordinary' taste) that was the 'New Thing' led to a sharp decline in interest in jazz of *all* kinds. Larkin is eloquently shrewd on this latter phenomenon in his *Weekend Telegraph* article of 23 April 1965, collected in Part Two below **[49]**.

42 The judgments deployed in these two sentences are strikingly original: no other jazz critic has made the same point.

43 Larkin spoke truer than he knew—or perhaps he *did* know. Almost as he wrote, LeRoi Jones was publishing *Blues People* (see **[33]**) and one of his acolytes, avant-garde tenor saxophonist Archie Shepp, would soon make the pronouncement, 'Whatever jazz is, I call it *mine*, baby.'

44 *Tempo* was the house magazine published by Boosey & Hawkes, the firm which by the 1930s was a 'leading international publisher of contemporary music' (Percy A. Scholes, *The Oxford Companion to Music*, tenth edition, 1991).

45 It is interesting how often Larkin wrote about Parker—supposedly, in Kingsley Amis's words when reviewing *All What Jazz*, 'his major hate and mine'. He

returns to him again and again in that book, and by no means always in hostile or even grudging vein; in this collection, too, the alto saxophonist is paid frequent and close attention. See particularly the review of 28 June 1973 and the *Weekend Telegraph* article that opens Part Two **[49]**.

46 See Note 29 above.

47 See Note 30 above.

48 See Note 26 above.

49 George Hoefer (1909–67) was a prolific writer on jazz and editor of *Down Beat* from 1958 to 1961.

50 This review was printed verbatim in an advertisement for the *Guardian* placed in *Jazz Journal*, December 1965 (xviii/12), 13.

51 Adam Clayton Powell, Jr. (1908–72) succeeded his father as pastor of the Abyssinian Baptist Church in New York City, and organised relief efforts and protests in Harlem during the Depression. Powell was elected to the city's council in 1941; in 1944 was elected to the United States House of Representatives from New York City, and served in that position until 1971. A flamboyant and controversial politician and preacher, Powell compiled a good voting record, but was increasingly criticized for making expensive foreign visits at public expense. Often quoted by Duke Ellington as an example of Harlem's 'godliness', Powell was eventually forced from office by congressional critics and revelations concerning his chequered private life.

52 It may be a surprise—and a cause for disagreement—to find Larkin placing Waller above both Johnson and Tatum in this fashion, but the authority of his musicological analysis is undeniable. Larkin was always perceptive about pianists.

53 It is worth recalling that Waller, strapped for cash, is reputed to have sold two of his finest songs—*The Sunny Side Of The Street* and *I Can't Give You Anything But Love*—to Jimmy McHugh, who has been credited with them ever since.

54 *Housewives' Choice* was a popular record-request programme during the 1950s and 1960s, broadcast on the BBC's Light Programme. It lapsed in 1967, when the Corporation's stations underwent wholesale reorganisation, including the launch of Radio One.

55 A felicitous example of Larkin's impatience with cant in general and wrongheaded jazz writing in particular. In 'How Am I To Know?' (2 February 1966, one of the most resonant of *All What Jazz*'s pieces) he wrote 'A critic is only as good as his ear', and he was ever suspicious of jazz criticism that failed to pay primary attention to the aural experience. The same irritated scorn underscores the final paragraph of this piece, especially its parting shot.

56 Ralph [Waldo] Ellison (1914–94), novelist and essayist, achieved literary fame with his novel *Invisible Man* (1952), in which the nameless protagonist moves from the racial conflicts of the agrarian South to those of the industrial North.

In 1965 a panel of critics judged *Invisible Man* the 'most distinguished fiction of the post-war period'.

57 Richard [Nathaniel] Wright (1908–1960), essayist and novelist, recounted his experiences of American racism in his autobiography *Black Boy* (1945) and the posthumously published *American Hunger* (1977). His novel *Native Son* (1940), the harrowing account of the life of Bigger Thomas, a black boy trapped by fear into the role of a 'brute killer', brought Wright critical acclaim. Always an 'outsider' because of his birth and experiences as an African-American, Wright went into self-imposed exile in Paris in 1946.

58 Charlie Christian revolutionised jazz guitar, partly through his innovative use of electrification and partly via his musical ideas, which, while rooted in swing, also heralded the advent of bop. Once a deeply impressed Benny Goodman had engaged him, he became nationally prominent, and would undoubtedly have become the first great bop guitarist had tuberculosis not claimed his life in 1942.

Perhaps the most interesting aspect of Ellison's reminiscence here is the impact of Lester Young on the young Christian. Young's crucial influence on bop and modern jazz has not received due critical attention. His *sound* may have seemed the most notable feature of his art, but his rhythmic conception was even more telling, for it affected musicians of all kinds, not just saxophonists. To learn that he exerted such an effect years before his famous debut with Count Basie is a valuable insight; its climactic inclusion here is characteristic of Larkin's acumen.

59 See Note 16 above.

60 It will be evident that Larkin admired McRae's book, and it is further praised in *All What Jazz* in the column printed on 10 July 1967, just three days after this piece. But the terse finality of his concluding remarks, especially the last three sentences, suggest increasing bewilderment with what the 'Wellses' profess to hear.

61 Those familiar with *All What Jazz* will recognise both tone and argument here. The latter has the not inconsiderable virtue of being correct, even if one's reaction to the results differs from the author's.

62 One of many instances in this collection when Larkin expresses—albeit obliquely in this case—disapproval of subsidising the arts.

63 The Eddie Marsh parallel is elaborated further in Larkin's review of Balliett's *Night Creature*. See **[45]** above, pages 101–5 and Note 80 below.

64 A superb aphorism that goes to the heart of Larkin's major reservations about Balliett, admiration for his style notwithstanding.

65 A favourite theme of Larkin's. Perhaps its most stirring incarnation is to be found in his *Telegraph* column of 15 June 1963.

66 LeRoi Jones (b. 1934), poet, novelist, short-story writer, essayist and music critic was born to black middle-class parents in Newark, New Jersey. In 1963

he published the influential study *Blues People: Negro Music In White America* (see Note 43 above). In 1965 Jones divorced his white wife and subsequently changed his name to Amiri Imamu Baraka. In the era of Black Power, Baraka embraced cultural nationalism and later became a Third-World Marxist-Leninist. In 1979 he joined the African Studies Department at the State University of New York, Stony Brook.

67 Another instance of stern critical priorities: as in his impatience at Charles Keil's sociological pamphleteering (see Note 55 above), Larkin has little time for polemic masquerading as musical analysis. And his unforgiving judgment has been vindicated in a specifically musical way: far from being transcendentally liberating, the 'New Thing' of the 1960s quickly proved a cul de sac, and a resort to exploring rock idioms would be needed before jazz rejoined the highway. The New Thing also—crowning irony in view of Jones's proselytising—turned African-Americans away from jazz; the majority of its enthusiasts were white Europeans.

68 This would not have been a popular judgment at the time; indeed, it is precisely the kind of remark that led many to dismiss Larkin as a commentator on jazz. Once again, however, Larkin has been vindicated. Mingus died in 1979, and in his last months was a forlorn figure—the pictures of him being comforted by President Jimmy Carter were uncommonly moving. The storms had not only died away but seemed forgotten, and while Mingus remains an important figure in jazz—not least through the magnificent Mingus Big Band, dedicated to preserving the spirit of his music—that durability is down to his work as practitioner, not protester.

69 Short for Extended Play. Containing the equivalent of two 7–inch singles and likewise played at 45 rpm, the EP benefited from the same microgroove technology as characterised the 10– or 12–inch Long Playing record.

70 See Note 12 above.

71 See Note 15 above.

72 This waspish remark is best understood in the light of Larkin's belief—some might say prejudice—that artists seldom have anything very interesting to say about their art. See, for example, the 13 June 1958 review of *Lady Sings The Blues* above, **[4]** where he comments, 'natural artists can rarely say anything enlightening about their own art . . . or of the changes in artistic fashion', or his remarks about Basie alumni in the 27 November 1980 review below. That is, presumably, why we need critics. (See Note 76 also.)

73 The brevity of this review of *Lady Sings The Blues* is both explained and countered by the longer one Larkin wrote in 1958. See **[4]** above, page 10.

74 The distinction between Porter's songs and Berlin's—or at least the way it is phrased—is very much a poet's perception.

75 Larkin reviewed *Owning Up* in the *Guardian*, 29 October 1965. See **[23]** above, pages 53–4.

76 This paragraph addresses two of the things that most irritated Larkin—sloppy writing and the notion that artists *necessarily* have anything of value to say about their art. See also Note 72 above.

77 In his *The Jazz Life* (London, 1964), Nat Hentoff records an analogous story at the end of his chapter on Basie, told by pianist Billy Taylor:

> One night at [the] Newport [Jazz Festival], I saw Bill off to one side, listening intently to a modern small combo. He was listening wistfully, it seemed to me. The group was pretty adventurous. Somebody interrupted Bill, and suddenly he was Count Basie again—the smile, the detachment. I just don't think he's as happy musically as he mostly convinces himself he is. There was more he wanted to do, but a while back, he decided to play it safe.

78 A leading theatre critic, Tynan was centrally involved in the creation of the National Theatre, whose first incarnation was at The Old Vic from 1963.

79 See Note 29 above.

80 (Sir) Edward (Howard) Marsh (1872–1953), civil servant, scholar and patron of the arts. His Civil Service career began in 1896 at the Colonial Office under Joseph Chamberlain, but he is best remembered as Winston Churchill's private secretary, a post he held for twenty-three years until the Labour victory of 1929. More germane in this instance are Marsh's activities as scholar, critic and anthologist. At Cambridge he had formed a close friendship with fellow 'Apostles' G. E. Moore and Bertrand Russell; later he came to the notice of (Sir) Edmund Gosse, who admitted him to his London literary circle. His first essays in criticism were notable for his championing of Ibsen and his catholic enthusiasm for poetry; in 1912 he wrote a critical appreciation of Rupert Brooke and in the same year published his anthology *Georgian Poetry*. He was equally taken with the (then) highly controversial work of Siegfried Sassoon, Robert Nichols and Robert Graves, and he was also instrumental in launching the career of Edmund Blunden.

   In his essay on Marsh for *The Dictionary of National Biography 1951–60* (ed. E. T. Williams and Helen M. Palmer, Oxford, 1971) Christopher Hassall writes, 'In spite of an abnormally acute aesthetic sensibility, [Marsh's] temperament was essentially methodical and rational, so that the one side of his nature was nicely balanced by the other, checking him from ever erring to an extreme on either side.' It was this judicious 'balance', perhaps, that triggered Bennett's irritation, which Larkin seems to share. However, it should not therefore be inferred that Larkin was in favour of 'erring to an extreme on either side': see Note 21 above, on F. R. Leavis and Sir John Squire.

81 See Note 30 above.

82 *Pace* the 'true life confessions' offered in the Introduction to *All What Jazz*, Larkin hardly ever indulged in 'reviewer-speak', but one suspects an instance here. For the 'situation' he has just finished describing is not so much

'paradoxical' as nonsensical: the notion that *anyone*'s prose, even Balliett's, can or indeed should make all jazzmen equally good is both preposterous and (to Larkin) fundamentally disagreeable. As he says in an earlier paragraph, 'a critic . . . likes some things and dislikes others, and finds reasons for doing so and for trying to persuade others to do so', and these final remarks, far from being the polite and amused whimsy they may seem, actually imply a prodigious narcissism on Balliett's part.

83 It is frankly sad to come across this hackneyed observation in what proved to be one of Larkin's last reviews of a jazz book. In his *Jazz: The Modern Resurgence* (London, 1990), Stuart Nicholson described Gillespie in highly comparable terms as remaining 'unromantically alive, almost a peripheral figure since the 1950s' (p. 78). Both critics thereby ignore—or are culpably oblivious of—Gillespie's wonderful work in the early 1960s with Lalo Schifrin, his renascence under the aegis of Norman Granz's Pablo label in the 1970s and the 1980s Indian summer basking in the glories of his United Nations Big Band. And while it is of course true that Gillespie will forever be primarily associated with the bop movement, those later achievements prompt the thought that, far from becoming enslaved by bop, he *transcended* it, and for that reason has claims to be considered a greater artist than Parker, albeit much less of an *influence* than his confrère. Time and again—in these pages and elsewhere —Larkin the jazz critic looked to challenge stale orthodoxy, and to find him resorting at the last to received unwisdom is regrettably unedifying.

84 A large claim, but there can be no doubt that Larkin meant every word of it. Thirteen years before, in 'Satchmo Still' (see **[35]**, pages 80–1) he had called Armstrong 'an artist of Flaubertian purity', and went on in even stronger terms: 'But has anyone yet seen him as the Chaucer, say, of the twenty-first century?' The heroic language is apt—if only because Armstrong was clearly Larkin's most enduring hero of all.

85 These two rhetorical questions express more than impatience: there is genuine anger here. Collier's book really *upset* Larkin, and the demolition of the book's inconsistency and tone has an unusual savagery beneath the characteristic suavity.

86 Max Jones and John Chilton, *Louis*, which Larkin reviewed in the *Guardian*, 21 October 1971 **[35]**.

87 This entire paragraph is as much a testament to the poet Larkin as to the jazz lover. The way he conjures up his own teenage 'bliss' in fewer than seventy words is comparable to the evocations of Sheffield railway station in 'Dockery and Son' or the gathering urban sprawl of London in 'The Whitsun Weddings'.

88 Reviewed by Larkin in the *Guardian*, 25 November 1976. See **[42]** above, pages 95–6.

89 Some might call the criticisms collected in these two paragraphs mere pedantry. But they again illustrate just how lovingly thorough and scholarly was Larkin's knowledge of the jazz scene.

90 Larkin is, of course, looking back to the early days of British jazz, and he is quite correct in suggesting that no English jazzman of real stature had emerged by the outbreak of World War II. But given the date of this piece's composition, it should be pointed out that by the early 1980s there was a host of native players of international standing: saxophonists John Surman and Ronnie Scott, pianists George Shearing and Victor Feldman (both born in England, even though they settled in America), bassist Dave Holland and drummer Martin Drew are just a few who come immediately to mind.

PART TWO

A Miscellany of Essays, Book Reports and Letters

Editors' note: *This miscellany is also presented chronologically. Superficially heterogeneous, the material is at all times underscored by Larkin's knowledge and love of jazz music; it also illuminates both his generosity and occasional toughness of judgment and his professional understanding of the economics of publishing. And the first item, a 1,500–word essay written four years into his stint as the* Daily Telegraph's *jazz correspondent, is nothing other than a buried masterpiece —certainly fit to rank with the Introduction to* All What Jazz, *and in several respects superior to it.*

49
Essay for *Weekend Telegraph*[1]

REQUIEM FOR JAZZ

... In a hundred years it grew from the slave-fields, captured the world, and at last split itself into two movements. Now both lie dying, writes PHILIP LARKIN, jazz correspondent for *The Daily Telegraph*—one unheard in the roar of 'beat', the other in the loneliness of chilly concert halls.

Charlie Parker, altoist extraordinary and father-figure of modern jazz, died ten years ago. The doctor said he had had a heart attack, the autopsy recorded lobar pneumonia. But in fact the Bird, who had ulcers, cirrhosis of the liver, and 'no veins left to inject', probably died, like Bix Beiderbecke, 'of everything'.[2]

He provoked legends. The beatniks who opt out of society in favour of the hypodermic and Zen idleness make him their patron saint—patient, dedicated, and way-out. To others he is the latest model of the self-destroying artist, the Rimbaud or Dylan Thomas who dies of too much ecstasy. They ignore hearsay that he was, alternately, a self-seeking treacherous charmer and a chaotic confused personality at the mercy of drink and drugs.[3]

But the biggest Parker legend is his place in jazz itself. To the younger generation, jazz began in the Forties with Charlie Parker, Dizzy Gillespie, Thelonious Monk and the rest: before that there was nothing but a desert of sentimentality and syncopation peopled with archaic figures such as Jelly Roll Morton and Benny Goodman. Bird the genius blew them all away with that four-bar break on 'A Night In Tunisia'.[4] The road was clear for grown-up jazz.

Technically, Parker *was* a genius. As a boy his playing had been publicly derided ('I went home and cried'), and as if in compensation he developed a staggering technique, jetting flurries of notes transcribable only as sixteenths, thirty-seconds, sixty-fourths. And he was a genius musically, in the sense that without any special education he instinctively felt his way to new harmonies, new rhythmic patterns, and showed how they could be used. Like all geniuses, he was imitated. By the time he died, aged 34 (the doctor put him down as 53), everything he had played was coming back to him.

He had touched off an explosion. The young Negro musician, brought up in the Roosevelt era, was bored with playing around with some dozen chords six nights a week. He resented that jazz had become, economically, a white man's music, and was impatient of the older players and their acceptance of the status of entertainer. His watchword became 'Make it something they can't steal,' both as a man and an artist turning his back on the audience. And Parker provided that something. Fumbling, he had felt his way out of the diatonic scale into chromaticism. For jazz, the way classical music had trodden some 50 years earlier suddenly lay open.[5]

The new impulse provided an enormous stimulus that is not yet spent. With the resources of musical theory to command, jazz set off in half a dozen different directions at once: novelty succeeded novelty, experiment splintered from experiment. Parker's bop was followed by Miles Davis's cool. The composers muscled in: Gunther Schuller, Gil Evans and George Russell[6] used classical instrumentation such as french horns and the new modes of atonality and the 12–tone scale. Others pushed improvisation further towards free form and complete anarchy: Ornette Coleman, who plays a white plastic saxophone and latterly violin (with his left hand), dispensed with pitch, chord progressions, and rhythm. There have been the Modern Jazz Quartet, drawing on early classical polyphony, and Dave Brubeck, teaching audiences to clap in 11/4 time.[7] All this has followed inevitably from Parker's innovations.

It has been approvingly called development. But there are different kinds of development: a hot bath can develop into a cold one. And in the excitement two things have been overlooked. Jazz is a popular art no longer. Also, it has disintegrated.

One has to compare Parker with Louis Armstrong to see precisely what has happened. Armstrong, too, had the experience of hearing everything he played come back to him, but his role had been different. Armstrong had been different. Armstrong had been the great integrator. Born in New Orleans in 1900, he had grown up to hear all the components of jazz melting into each other and by bringing them into the focus of his own definitive style, had created the jazz language. People have said that Armstrong brought nothing new to jazz. But no other trumpet strikes out of those early pre-electric records in quite the way Armstrong's does.[8] He gave jazz its speaking voice, and it was heard all over the world.

How can one account for it, the universality of jazz? What did it hold that conquered pretty well every capital city in the world? Something to do with the hybrid nature of the music, no doubt, the union of Europe and Africa, the waltzes and hymns. There was excitement in it, and release, and a wish to start dancing. But above all there was happiness: people listening to jazz were on good terms with themselves. 'I enjoy playing for people that are happy,' said veteran New Orleans trombone player Jim Robinson. 'It gives me a warm heart and that gets into my music . . . Everyone in the world should know this.'[9]

They did. Right through the Twenties and Thirties, no matter whether it is Armstrong, the alcoholic evanescent Bix, the killer-diller mechanics of Benny Goodman, or Lester Young incongruously elliptic and a little world-weary against the boisterous Basie band, the excitement and the happiness held good. Proclaimed everywhere by records, radio and films, jazz became the emotional language of the century.

But it was Armstrong's jazz. And when one listens to what succeeded it, to what came out of America at the end of the war—Parker's jazz—and, still more, to the many different modes we have today, it is hard to see it as other than a wilful inversion, not a development at all. It is not so much the stylistic changes—the abandonment of collective improvisation, making the last chorus a frigid unison repetition of the first; the classical intonation; the rhythmic emphases purposely at variance with those of the dance—as the total reversal of spirit and message. Where there had been joy and relaxation, there was now tension and antagonism.[10] If in traditional jazz, neurosis had been balanced by a vital innocence, as Wilfrid Mellers says in *Music in a New Found Land*, 'now only the neurosis is left.'[11] Armstrong, in one of his rare outbursts against fellow musicians, termed it 'that modern malice . . . no melody to remember and no beat to dance to', and perhaps malice, the malice of the modern American Negro, was what it was.

Jazz had become self-conscious, artistically as well as socially: hence the chromaticism, the language of the minority artist. The fact that it is a commonplace in classical music doesn't alter the fact that the popular ear was and still is a diatonic ear: if you want a hymn, a lullaby, a love song, or simply a tune to whistle, chromaticism is no use. Admittedly these may not be the highest kind of music. But they are the kind jazz was.

The composite picture this adds up to is of a folk-music swept by the unique nature of its appeal to the point where it is exhausted by over-exploitation, made self-conscious by political feeling and technical sophistication, and deprived of its natural participating audience in exchange for the concert hall, the subsidised festival, the college circuit.[12] It can be regarded, particularly in its sillier moments, as an art that has travelled from the Lascaux cave paintings[13] to Picasso in 50 giddy years. And its practitioners have taken just 50 years to reach the point where they turn their backs on the audience. What we have increasingly—and what we shall have completely when some few dozen of the old cave-painters are gone, Armstrong and Ellington, Hodges and Clayton, Ben Webster and Henry Allen—is a dreary ante-chapel of modern-art music, and this will be no substitute for the passionate speech we have lost.[14]

But perhaps what clinches this central diagnosis is the sudden, recent and extravagant vogue for 'beat' music. It doesn't take much imagination to see that this is where the jazz impulse, the jazz following, has migrated. This is where the jazz public has gone, and even where jazz has gone, for this music, rock and roll, rhythm and blues, or just plain beat, is for all its tedious vulgarity nearer jazz than the rebarbative astringencies of Coleman, Coltrane and the late Eric Dolphy.[15]

To say Parker destroyed jazz as well as himself would be the crudest of generalisations, and would imply that what has happened, the 'development', could have been averted. Very likely it couldn't. Jazz was a unique phenomenon, set off by an unprecedented balance of sociological factors—in the same way as, shall we say, the Border ballads—which are now dissipating and will not recur. The music Parker split in two is now vanishing simultaneously into the vulgarities of popular entertainment, and will soon be a historical memory, like ragtime.[16] The world will have lost that incredible argot that in the first half of the 20th century spoke to all nations and all intelligences equally.[17]

23 April 1965

Editors' note: *the article was illustrated by three photographs by Art Kane—of Louis Armstrong, Duke Ellington and Lester Young.*

50

Thesis Report for the Library Association

A GUIDE TO THE LITERATURE OF JAZZ by Donald L. Kennington, ALA

> My aim in producing this guide is to indicate to the beginner in jazz which are
> the significant works and to refresh the memory of the expert as to the books
> he has probably read in the past. I also hope to be able to indicate to the librarian
> both the books and journals he needs to stock in order to achieve a balanced
> collection and the sources he might try when locating information on the
> subject. (p. vii)

That is Mr Kennington's definition of the purpose of his work, and he
fulfils it admirably. I have read his thesis with great interest: he refers to
most of the books I know (and to a lot I don't!) and I found his sections on
'The Periodical Literature' and 'Organisations' most informative. At the
same time his work does not do more than he claims for it. The literature
of jazz is a fugitive business, and an index to it would be a much vaster and
more specialised work than this. Mr Kennington is well aware of this, as
the opening paragraph of Ch. 6 makes clear. All the same, his selection
('the work ... is selective', p.vii) is accurate, informed and thorough. I
conclude that Mr Kennington knows his subject in detail ('the author has
been interested in this field since 1946', p.x), and his acknowledgements
suggest that he is at home in its international context.

My criticisms are few. Bibliographically, I wonder why he so rigorously
eschews forenames, even when they are known (Feather, L., for instance,
or Fox, C.). His list of abbreviations (p. xii) does not flatter the reader—do
we really need to be told that M.A. stands for Master of Arts, or pseud. for

pseudonym? The lack of conventional collation (number of pages, illustrations, etc.) suggests that he has not examined the items he records, though I don't think this is admitted. The entry 'NEWTON, F. *pseud.*' (p. 31) might well have included his real name, which is well enough known (E. J. Hobsbawm). There are a few minor carelessnesses: 'wax works' (p. 158) is waxworks (p. 175). The acute accent on Hugues Panassié is omitted, though accents are occasionally marked on other words. The Corgi edition of *We Called It Music* (p. 80) in fact has a new discography by Dave Carey. Here and there are mis-spellings (paralleling, p.223). He has an irritating habit of using both italics and quotation marks ('*Jazz Scene*', p.15).

Jazzwise, there is equally little to quarrel with. Mr Kennington's opinions seem what is conventionally accepted. I doubt, however, if *Young Man With a Horn* appeared (p. 68) eight years after its subject's death: Beiderbecke died in 1931. I believe the popular legend of Bessie Smith's 'extremely tragic death' (p. 92) has been exploded. The reiterated charge (pp. 185–6, 206) that *Vintage Jazz Mart* is unreadable by reason of its type size is an exaggeration. Sometimes Mr Kennington seems over-ready to accept a book's claims: the discography of *Treat It Gentle* (p. 67) is not, I believe, complete—discographies hardly ever are!

Intellectually, or perhaps stylistically, Mr Kennington suggests a painstaking but ordinary mind, ready to adopt any cliché that comes to hand and not particularly original in thought or phraseology. It is only this characteristic that restrains me from suggesting that he turn this thesis into a commercially publishable work: it would certainly be welcome for the information it contains.

I think there can be no doubt that this thesis should be accepted. The minor nature of my criticisms may suggest to you that it might be worthy of special distinction.

June 1969

51

Letter Concerning *The Literature of Jazz*

Mr Kennington's thesis (see [50]) *was duly accepted; two years later it was published. On reading an unflattering four-line review in the* Times Literary Supplement, *Larkin wrote to that journal in protest: the letter was published in the edition of 26 March 1971, along with a reply from the (anonymous) reviewer.*

'The Literature of Jazz'

Your reviewer of Donald Kennington's *The Literature of Jazz* (March 12) does himself and the book scant justice in saying that it 'has no decisive aim'. This is set out on the first page of the introduction:

> My aim . . . is to indicate to the beginner in jazz which are the significant works and to refresh the memory of the expert as to the books he has probably read in the past. I also hope to be able to indicate to the librarian both the books and journals he needs to stock in order to achieve a balanced collection and the sources he might try when locating information on the subject.

Presumably your reviewer has heard of a critical bibliography before. That is what Mr. Kennington's book is: unadventurous in its opinions, perhaps, and inelegantly written, if you like, but as thorough and accurate in its coverage as the imprint of the Library Association would suggest.

Philip Larkin

All Souls College, Oxford OX1 4AL

*** Our reviewer writes:—'There is a great deal of difference between stating an aim and achieving it. The implication of my review was that Mr.

Kennington's brief critical assessments might mislead the beginner (*vide* his comments on Max Harrison's book about Parker). But I did not question Mr. Kennington's conscientiousness: I merely said that I thought the job had not been done very well. Mr. Larkin may think that this is a critical bibliography which can be recommended: I don't, despite the lack of rivals in this field.'[18]

52

Book Report for Oxford University Press

THE JAZZ TRADITION by Martin Williams

Mr Williams is a well-known jazz writer (principally of journalism—he is a regular contributor to *Down Beat*—but he has edited at least one collection of essays, 'The Art Of Jazz', published here by Cassell), now in his mid-forties and a recognised name in the American jazz world.

Mr Williams says 'I hope from the chapters that follow, two ideas will emerge of how jazz evolved. One has to do with the position of certain major figures and what they have contributed to jazz. The other has to do with rhythm.' The first of these ideas comes over better than the second—in fact, I wasn't conscious of any contentions about rhythm at all.[19] His major figures are Morton, Armstrong, Beiderbecke, Hawkins, Holiday, Ellington, Basie, Young, Parker, Monk, John Lewis, Sonny Rollins, Horace Silver, Coltrane and Ornette Coleman. Of these, John Lewis and Horace Silver might seem a little over-parted[20] by inclusion, but he makes a case for them. In every essay Mr Williams gives an account of the work of his subject and its place in the history of jazz; his remarks are well supported by reference to recordings, and always contain some suggestions about the nature of the work in question which are interesting and seemingly original. This is not a technical book, from a musical point of view, but Mr Williams is clearly well enough grounded in the art to make a technical point where necessary.

Mr Williams knows more about jazz than I do, and I hesitate to criticize anything he says. Two reservations I make are, first, that there seems little continuity or theme in the book, except that of the chronological order of its subjects; secondly, I am not sure if Mr Williams is sufficiently distinguished enough (*sic*) as a writer (and perhaps a thinker) to be published by the Press.[21] Neither of these points will prevent his book being published in this country, and being popular, but a perusal of his first chapter will show what I mean.

January 1970

The following extracts from Larkin's covering letter to Jonathan Crowther of OUP, 14 March 1970, are also germane

. . . the book lacks a final conclusory chapter, in which the all-too-invisible threads of his argument would be drawn together, and I seem to miss the quality of a good mind behind what he writes generally.

If you don't publish the book, I am sure someone else will . . . [22]

YOUR JAZZ COLLECTION by Derek Langridge (Clive Bingley, 40s)

This book is intended for the jazz collector, though its author hopes that it will be of use to the librarian faced—as Mr Langridge urges he should increasingly be—with the job of arranging and indexing jazz literature and records. Mr Langridge is both a principal lecturer at the North Western Polytechnic and a life-long jazz enthusiast, so he is well qualified to deal with his subject.

The first half of the book is taken up with a disquisition on collecting in general and jazz collecting in particular, and on 'collector's aids'. The first of these seems somewhat discursive, taking in such matters as 'The psychology of record length' and a parallel between the lyrics of 'You Always Hurt the One You Love' and *The Ballad of Reading Gaol*, but it does lead ultimately to the assertion of Mr Langridge's belief (which I share) that 'an Englishman who had heard every performance by visiting American musicians would still have heard very little. The real jazz lover must be a record collector.'[23] The second chapter is a survey of dis-cographies, bibliographies and other works of reference, together with more general examples of jazz literature: this shows a thorough and extensive knowledge that gives the reader confidence in his guide.

The second, and without doubt more original, half of the book is taken up with attempting to solve the problem of how to arrange and index jazz books and records. Mr Langridge treats the two media separately—that is, the same method will not do for both—and neither has any relation to any existing scheme of classification. His 'Classification for the literature of jazz' is buttressed by an index and two sample lists of real books and periodical articles classified according to the scheme. It consists of twenty divisions, each nominated by a letter of the alphabet and sub-divided alphabetically once or even twice. Some divisions are subject divisions, some are form divisions: some can be either. B (Reference works) has the subdivision Bg (Discographies), where Rust's *Jazz Records 1897 to 1931* could be placed, but a discography of Charlie Parker would go at Spar BG (S is *Writings on individual musicians* divided by the first letters of their names). One cannot criticize a subject division in a few lines, but I was surprised to find a section 'T: Afro-American Music'—I had rather supposed this was what jazz was—and to find within that section, which turns out to be devoted to blues, folk and soul, the mode of ragtime: very different, I should have thought, spiritually, chronologically, musically, and in every other way.[24]

As regards records, Mr Langridge admits that most people arrange them as far as they can by name of principal performer, and that this way 'is certainly more useful than either of the other methods discussed', but he none the less goes on to expound arrangements by style and period, and closes with a demonstration of the usefulness of an index in uniting different takes and different sessions which may be scattered far and wide through numerous physical discs.

It can be said in Mr Langridge's favour that, first, he is bringing order to a scene notorious for conflicting methods and unscholarly approaches and, second, what he proposes is based on his arrangement and indexing of his own collection, and so can be shown to have worked in at least one case. Certainly jazz collectors should study his advice and judge whether or not they think it will profit them.

December 1970

54
Letter to Terry Henebery

In 1971 Larkin was asked by Terry Henebery, a leading freelance television producer with a particular interest in jazz (he had been responsible for BBC2's important series 'Jazz 625' in the mid–1960s) to join a panel of authorities to document the history of jazz for a special programme. Larkin's reply was sent on 30 September 1971.

Dear Mr. Henebery,

Thank you for your letter of the 25th September. I am sorry not to have taken your telephone call—in fact, I hadn't realised it was you who was calling: your name got through to me as Hanbury. Of course, like all jazz lovers, I have known and enjoyed your work for a long time.

Regarding your proposal: while grateful for the suggestion, I really doubt whether I am an eminent authority on jazz, as you so flatteringly put it. I am really no more than someone who has always liked jazz, and who was lucky enough more or less by accident to be asked to review records for *The Daily Telegraph*, which I have been doing since 1961 (you may have seen a collection of my reviews, *All What Jazz*, Faber 1970). I have never been able to claim the real specialised knowledge of the record collector or the jazz historian or the musicologist. All I have (on my good days) is an ability to write smart journalism that makes the record sound attractive or unattractive as the case may be.[25]

Secondly, I am a timid and retiring person, and rarely appear on radio and never on television. This is mostly due to shyness, but also because I have so much to do already I can't really spare the time such projects seem to demand. If, therefore, you were thinking of my actually appearing in your project, as distinct from writing a script or selecting a programme of records, then I am afraid I should not be a good prospect.

Now you have the above information, you may like to reconsider whether I should be as useful to you as you at first supposed. I shan't be at all offended if you decide in the negative. If you still think there is anything in it for either of us, perhaps we might, as you suggest, meet for further discussion.[26]

With all good wishes,

Yours sincerely,

55
Book Report for Faber & Faber

BLACK BEAUTY, WHITE HEAT: A PICTORIAL HISTORY OF CLASSIC JAZZ, 1920–1950 by Franklin S. Driggs and Harris Lewine

[To Patrick Carnegy]

Thank you for sending me a copy of this book. It must be conceded at the outset that it *is* a remarkable collection of jazz photographs, many of which are unfamiliar to me, and it will certainly become a milestone in this rather esoteric area of jazz appreciation. Inevitably one compares it with Keepnews and Grauer's *A Pictorial History of Jazz* (1960),[27] and without counting I should say that it contains a great many more photographs, as well as the additional reproductions of record labels, sheet music covers, concert programmes, magazines and other ephemerae. Driggs and Lewine have made a richer and longer book, and the quality of the reproductions is much better.

At the same time, it suffers in comparison by its very inclusiveness. Compared with Keepnews and Grauer, the photographs are crowded together, some of them being too small for the amount of detail they contain, and in the interests of saving space the captions to all of them are run together at the bottom of the page, which makes immediate identification noticeably difficult. Driggs and Lewine have also eschewed the occasional dramatic blow-up (such as the death certificate of Bix Beiderbecke) which made the earlier book so exciting. The layout, too, with its omnipresent ruled borders, seems fussy and dated.

I enclose a review of the book by an editor of the traditional jazz magazine *Storyville*, which is typical of the enthusiastic reception the book will get among the *aficionados*, but I think it should be realised that these people constitute a minority within a minority. I also enclose a page from the same magazine making it clear that *Storyville* is already importing copies of *Black Beauty, White Heat* at £26, and a friend of mine who has tried to buy one has been told they are already sold out. I think in other words that the people who will be prepared to put down £25 for this book are not very numerous, and they will probably get their copies somehow without your intervention. It is, as I think I said in an earlier letter, the kind of book one sees remaindered, for all its excellences.[28]

I hope I may keep the copy you sent, as fee for the consultation.[29]

December 1982

56

Essay on Duke Ellington in *Makers of Modern Culture*

MAKERS OF MODERN CULTURE edited by Justin Wintle (Routledge & Kegan Paul, 1981)

In addition to being accorded an entry in his own right (written by Valentine Cunningham), Larkin wrote two appraisals for Wintle's survey. To reprint here the essay on John Betjeman would not be appropriate, but its characteristic mixture of authoritative generosity and acute insight is mirrored in his assessment of Ellington. It is perhaps surprising that Larkin was not also entrusted with the entry on his beloved Louis Armstrong, which went instead to Christopher Wagstaff.

ELLINGTON, DUKE 1899–1974

US jazz composer

Edward Kennedy 'Duke' Ellington, as his nickname implies, brought distinction to jazz. Partly it was social distinction, taking the American Negro's music into Carnegie Hall, Westminster Abbey and the White House, but primarily it was musical distinction: the creation of a substantial body of work that challenged comparison with that of modern European composers without losing touch with its own indigenous origins.

Ellington was a pianist who composed for the jazz orchestra he led. Born in 1899, he had a five-piece band by 1923, which attained a distinctive character with the addition of growl-trumpeter 'Bubber' Miley in 1925. Accompanying floor-shows at the Cotton Club after 1927 developed his 'jungle music' image with *Black and Tan Fantasy* and *The Mooche*, balanced by more lyrical pieces such as *Creole Love Call* and *Mood Indigo*. He began recording in 1924, and when he visited Europe in 1933 it was to find himself famous. His music was already evolving: *Reminiscin' in Tempo* (1935) showed that Ellington had already listened to Ravel, Debussy and Delius, with whom he had already been compared. But his compositions lost none of their excitement; by 1940 his superb orchestra had reached another peak with *Ko-Ko, Harlem Airshaft* and many others.

The individuality of Ellington's music lay in his adaptation of the jazz idiom to impressionist moods, and in the originality of his scoring, but he depended heavily on a long line of inventive soloists (Miley, Joe Nanton, Johnny Hodges, Cootie Williams), some of whom stayed with him for decades. In 1939 he recruited the arranger Billy Strayhorn, and a remarkable collaboration ensued until the latter's death in 1967, so that the responsibility for any 'Ellington' piece was never entirely clear.[30]

During the second half of his career his repertoire became more extended. His stature as a Negro composer was increased by the suites *Black Brown and Beige* and *New World A-Comin'* (both 1943), but his post-war inter-continental travels produced *The Far East Suite* (1964) and *The Latin-American Suite* (1968). There were also the three Sacred Concerts (San Francisco 1965, New York 1968 and London 1973) that were repeated all over Europe. His orchestra never abandoned its jazz character, however, and maintained a gruelling schedule of commercial engagements till within a few months of Ellington's death in 1974.

The range and originality of Ellington's music brought him world-wide acclaim. Paradoxically, his recordings are permanent masterpieces, but their scores are neglected or lost, and in any case could not be played by another group. Despite the ambition of his concert pieces, he was most successful as a miniaturist; the suites have undeniable *longueurs*. As his greatest soloists aged or fell away, some of the excitement waned, but Ellington himself, disregarding post-Parker experiments, maintained his tireless creativity and his orchestra's unique timbre. André Previn said that whereas most arranged jazz could be analysed, 'Duke merely lifts his finger, three horns make a sound, and I don't know what it is'. Or as Ellington himself said, more simply, 'The band you run has got to please the audience. The band I run has got to please me.'

The Works of Duke Ellington (French RCA) is a variorum edition of Ellington's recordings for Victor; *The Complete Duke Ellington* (CBS) does the same for his work on other labels such as Columbia and Brunswick. Numerous selections have been issued. *Duke Ellington's Story on Records*

1925–45 by Luciano Massagli and others (5 vols, Milan 1966) is an exhaustive discography for the period indicated; J. G. Jepsen's *Jazz Records 1942–65: Vol 3 Co-El* (Denmark 1967) provides further guidance. See also: Stanley Dance, *The World of Duke Ellington* (1971); Duke Ellington, *Music Is My Mistress* (1974) and Derek Jewell, *Duke: a Portrait of Duke Ellington* (1977).

Part Two: Notes

1 *Weekend Telegraph* was a colour supplement magazine that accompanied the paper on Fridays.

2 While the Beiderbecke–Parker parallel is deft, a mischievous reader might reflect that both here and elsewhere Larkin seems to link Parker's self-destructiveness to the music he made rather more than attends his analysis of the cornetist. In addition, the vinegary 'Zen idleness' and the thinly veiled impatience of 'dies of too much ecstasy' signal a moral response absent in Larkin's masterly piece on Beiderbecke for the *New Statesman* written nine years later ([41], pages 92–94). That said and maybe felt, Larkin once again has the considerable virtue of being right. Bebop may not have been able to count the invention of the self-destructive artist amongst its innovations, but the casualty list of modern jazzmen (and women) is a hideously lengthy matter of record.

3 See Larkin's reviews of Reisner and Russell on Parker in Part One above ([20] and [39]).

4 To be found on **Portrait of the Bird**, Columbia 33SX 1555 (UK LP). Larkin reviewed the album—very warmly—in the *Daily Telegraph*, 13 November 1963.

5 Relevant here is the very interesting *Serious Music and All That Jazz* by Henry Pleasants, published by Gollancz in 1969 and reviewed by Larkin in September of that year (*All What Jazz*, 236–7). In an earlier book, *Death of A Music?*, Pleasants had lamented the demise of classical music into something few wanted to listen to any longer, and now he expressed the same concern over jazz. Paraphrasing Pleasants's case, Larkin observed—in terms corresponding exactly to the thesis of *Requiem for Jazz*—that it has become 'a private music unsupported by popular approval, and died the death'.

6 Schuller (b. 1925), a distinguished writer on jazz as well as a composer of note, was with John Lewis, J. J. Johnson and others centrally involved in the first 'Third Stream' projects, which, as Larkin implies, sought to marry the worlds of jazz and classical music. The recently reissued **Birth of the Third Stream** (Columbia Legacy 485103 2) includes two Schuller works, *Symphony for Brass and Percussion* and *Transformation*. Evans (1912–88) is chiefly renowned for his collaborations with Miles Davis (amongst them **Miles Ahead** and **Porgy And Bess**), but his work elsewhere was hardly less seminal, notably two albums for Impulse!, **Out of the Cool** and **Into the Hot** and a magnificent date for Verve in 1964, **The Individualism of Gil Evans**. The 'modes of atonality and the 12–tone scale' that Larkin cites are perhaps most germane to the work of Russell (b. 1923), especially his **Jazz Workshop** sessions in the mid–1950s (RCA). More recently, Russell wrote the exhilarating **African Game** (Blue Note) and with his Living Time Orchestra is now exploring a synthesis of many forms.

7 The only piece in 11/4 time that Brubeck ever recorded was the eponymous 'Eleven-Four' that appears on Volume Two of **Dave Brubeck At Carnegie Hall** (Columbia: LP only at present). Larkin never reviewed the album for the *Telegraph* or anyone else; his witty *en passant* flick quietly testifies to how dense and up-to-date was his knowledge of recorded jazz, even the work of those he professed to have little time for.

8 These two sentences have a resonance and import out of all proportion to their length, for they address head-on the vexed question of 'innovation' and its true status in a music that from the start drew heavily on already established European tradition, even if its rhythmic élan was both revolutionary and unique. From the outset jazz criticism has been obsessed with 'Who did it first?' in a fashion not to be found in any other art form; moreover, the issue is often approached in an aurally deadened and near-puerile way. Larkin is surely right both to concede that Armstrong brought nothing *obviously* 'new' to jazz and to stress the much more important point that his work was and remains incomparably superior to anything that had gone before. And if differences in taste mean that one cannot quite concur with Larkin's implication that no one rivalled Armstrong afterwards either, his argument is as vigorous as refreshing.

9 Robinson's delightful remark irresistibly recalls Larkin's own definition of jazz and how to recognise it in the *Telegraph* column 'Credo' of February 1967:

> I can recognise jazz because it makes me tap my foot, grunt affirmative exhortations, or even get up and caper round the room. If it doesn't do this … it isn't jazz.

No definition of jazz can be perfect—both the word and the music are too slippery. But Larkin's effort here is more than decent. The only problem is that he uses it to canonise his own favourites—Armstrong, Beiderbecke and so on—at the direct exclusion of all others. But it isn't *that* much of a problem, because the whole thing quickly reduces to a matter of semantics. That definition of his exactly captures how anyone might feel about his/her special favourites, and it doesn't really signify how this or that purist wants to label the music at issue. It is, as Larkin and Robinson both stress, the *joy* that matters.

10 Larkin argues this familiar stance forcefully at all times, and to a considerable extent what he says here is right. But there is another side to bop, or rather a different way of seeing and hearing it, and there is no better advocate than Ira Gitler in his 1985 *Swing To Bop* (Oxford University Press, 1985, 310):

> In assessing the impact of bebop there are several aspects to be considered. One was 'the war to make the world safe for democracy', as people were calling it. It was a fight against the Nazis and the forces of Fascism which represented bigotry and oppression. A black author, Roi Ottley, wrote a book called *New World 'A Comin'*, and many black people did feel that life would be better for them after World War II.
>
> There was a hopefulness expressed in (Bebop) whether it was conscious or not. It had joy, beauty and optimism.

Looked at in such a light, bop is less a music of 'tension and antagonism' than a noble expression of the Pleasure Principle. That, it could be argued, informs all that is best in civilisation; certainly, it prompted the Irish poet Michael Longley, writing in the *Observer* of 27 August 1995, to argue that

> Jazz is an antidote to authoritarianism. That's why its emergence in the century of the jackboot is of the greatest cultural importance—it's the twentieth century's most significant contribution to the culture of the world. Syncopation is the opposite of the goose step.

11 Wilfrid Mellers, *Music In A New Found Land: Themes and Developments in the History of American Music* (London: Barrie & Rockliff, 1964).

12 These cogent observations about the changes in locale remind one that by this time (1965) the jazz clubs—those precious nurseries—were in rapid decline in the USA and would never recover, a pattern that was reflected globally.

But Larkin's remarks also call to mind some comments made by Derek Jewell during his 1970 review of *All What Jazz*. His case is all the more telling for having been made so seldom—if ever—by anyone else:

> There is rarely any feeling that [Larkin] has actually *seen* the people he writes about performing in the flesh. And even though the sight of Miles Davis in concert would scarcely make Mr Larkin love this strange genius more, exposure to the artist-audience experience is as much a part of insight into jazz as impressions stamped on wax. (Philip Larkin Papers: Brynmor Jones Library, University of Hull, cited hereafter as PLPBJL.)

Also germane here is Larkin to Kingsley Amis, 23 September 1979, in which, referring to Steve Race's autobiography (see **[43]**), he notes: 'I was pleased to see that what finally put him off jazz was *live performances*. Couldn't stand the drums solos, and the bass solos . . . Right, eh?' (*Selected Letters*, 605).

13 The earliest paintings in the Lascaux caves in France 'seem to date from about 15,000 B.C. . . . For sheer vitality, freedom of hand and sureness of touch, the best of these paintings have rarely been excelled.' That is the judgment of Hugh Honour and John Fleming in their *A World History of Art* (King; rev. edn. 1995, 7); their epithets could all but describe the early jazz that Larkin loved so much, and thus point up the appositeness of his analogy.

14 In a precise if narrow sense, this last claim is not true. That 'passionate speech' Larkin is mourning remains logged on record—these days, thanks to digital remastering and other new techniques, more faithfully than ever before. A quick look back to the end of his *New Statesman* review-article on Bix Beiderbecke (see **[41]** pages 92–94) finds Larkin making the same point, if less than celebratorily, in his last two sentences:

> When the Depression lifted, Bix, and the world of white jazz he had inspired, were gone: the future lay with Goodman and his Henderson scores. Only the indestructible delight of his records remains. (See page 94 above.)

15 Not all will agree with Larkin's analysis here; however, in his (unpublished) 1988 University of Brighton dissertation *Sonny Rollins: The Search For Self Through Art*, Michael Jackson observes that the mid-to-late 1960s witnessed 'jazz's worst slump in its fifty years of recorded history', citing 'post-avant-garde shock and the advent of rock' as twin causes. Implicit in Jackson's words is a notion Larkin here makes explicit—that the two phenomena were symbiotically connected. Notwithstanding the 'tedious vulgarity' that Larkin cites, rock was in some respects nearer to the spirit of jazz than earnest experimentalism. Its beat may have been anodyne, but people could dance to it with easy pleasure: nobody danced to the strains of Ornette Coleman or John Coltrane. And no matter how trivial, the melodies of 1960s' rock were instantly singable and stayed in the memory: as Larkin observes in the previous paragraph of *Requiem for Jazz*, 'the popular ear . . . is a diatonic ear'.

16 As in his earlier remark concerning the loss of 'the passionate speech' of early jazz, this is not strictly true (see Note 14 above). There has been, since Larkin's death in 1985, a distinct revival of interest in ragtime, reflected in the profusion of reissues and indeed new recordings of the genre. While one naturally takes Larkin's 'historical' point, those records ensure that ragtime will remain an active and valued part of twentieth-century music, and to propose that it has vanished into antiquarian memory is akin to suggesting

that the poetry of (say) Marvell or Pope has been entirely eclipsed by that of Yeats, Eliot and Auden.

17 Throughout his work, Larkin was hardly ever sentimental, but he is uncomfortably close to it in this last sentence. He had paddled in such perilous waters in his review of Benny Green's *The Reluctant Art* (see **[18]** above, pages 40–41) when concluding

> What was so exciting about jazz was the way its unique, simple gaiety instantly communicated itself to such widely differing kinds of human being—Negro porters, Japanese doctors, King George VI

and this later assertion finds him not waving but drowning. The case is badly overstated, and its crudeness could threaten to undermine his core-argument concerning the subsequent fragmentation of jazz music.

18 An intriguing albeit minor question arises from this diverting 'tiff'. Kennington's critical bibliography is no longer an 'active' title in the literature of jazz, and indeed few aficionados of our acquaintance had ever heard of it. So who was 'right'—Larkin or the anonymous *TLS* reviewer?!

19 This apparently sweeping claim is entirely justified. Williams offers a number of *observations* about rhythm and/or descriptions of how certain players approached it (the 1930s Count Basie Orchestra, for example), but these do not amount to governingly systematic 'contentions'.

20 A somewhat arcane term, 'over-parted' means 'having too difficult a part to play'. The suggestion is that Lewis and Silver seem lightweight in such company.

21 An apparently lordly judgment that underlines Larkin's dissatisfaction at anything he perceives as second-rate. It would seem that the Press did not agree, or else did not find Larkin's reservations decisive enough to prohibit adopting the book (see Note 22 below). Those interested in supporting evidence for Larkin's view might consult Williams's final book, *Hidden In Plain Sight* (OUP, 1992).

22 Oxford University Press duly published Williams's book. A new and revised edition of *The Jazz Tradition* appeared in 1983.

23 The second sentence quoted could almost be construed as a 'Larkin manifesto'. See Note 12 above, and also the Introduction.

24 Larkin disliked sloppy thinking as much as sloppy writing, and his impatience here is all the more striking in the context of an otherwise very favourable review.

25 If not exactly disingenuous, these two sentences do not convince. There is almost spectacularly more to Larkin's record reviews than 'smart journalism', and the pieces collected in this volume evince a 'specialised knowledge' as dense as profound. Larkin may not have been a professional 'musicologist', but taken together *All What Jazz* and *Jazz Writings* show him to have been a

'jazz historian' of the first rank. Terry Henebery would not have been interested in him otherwise, and Larkin's modest words seem chiefly predicated on a desire to say 'no', for reasons outlined in the subsequent paragraph.

26 The correspondence seems to have ended at this point, and we therefore infer that Henebery did not follow up the suggestion in Larkin's final paragraph.

27 See above, Part One, Note 31.

28 A quiet reminder of Larkin the expert librarian—a man as thoroughly at home with the economics and 'business' of books as with their aesthetic dimension.

29 It is not clear from Carnegy's response whether Faber & Faber planned to adopt the book; it would seem that in the event they did not.

30 Like every other judgment in his essay, Larkin's observation here has proved as durable as judicious. In his excellent recent biography of Strayhorn, *Lush Life* (New York: Farrar, Straus & Giroux, 1997), David Hadju notes that 'on stage, Ellington referred to Strayhorn with cryptic aesthetic intimacy as "our writing and arranging companion" ' (121), and in his confessed inability at times to identify precisely which 'bits' of a collaborative composition were whose, Hadju further suggests that in more than a few instances not even the collaborators themselves could have done so.

PART THREE

Daily Telegraph Records of the Year, 1961–70

Polls of any kind are both trivial and ephemeral, and it would be unwise to read all that much into these annual reflections. On the other hand, some of Larkin's choices are striking, especially to those who know Larkin as jazz critic mainly via the Introduction to All What Jazz. The praise for Mingus and Adderley is notable, as is the selection of 'Miles in The Sky' in both 1968 and 1969; on one level, that duplication may be considered a careless oversight, but the choice is hardly less eloquent as a result. Above all, however, it is the 1964 inclusion of Coltrane's 'A Love Supreme' and Coleman's 'Chappaqua Suite' in 1968 that stand out.

There are three possible ways of responding to this. Two of them hold little water—the notion that Larkin secretly liked such music much more than he let on in his monthly Telegraph columns, and the suggestion that he completed these 'Record of the Year' returns in a mood of pure cynicism commensurate with his famous 'jazz whore' confession (All What Jazz, 18–19). The first is patently untenable, and the second no less unlikely despite a surface plausibility. Larkin makes his personal enthusiasms abundantly clear, and in other instances his tone is judiciously alert, without even the hint of a sneer, let alone any meretricious posturing.

The third possibility is that, like the properly responsible critic that he was, Larkin used these pieces to draw attention to the current state of the art as he saw it. As noted, in virtually every case he distinguishes between 'personal favourites' and records which he recognises as important even if they are not to his taste. Few jazz critics have been as disinterested in such circumstances; few, too, have been that prescient or durable in their judgments. Over a generation on, no serious jazz enthusiast could claim that any of Larkin's choices was inflated or misguided, and the majority of them are recognised as essential.

57
1961 (18 December 1961)

My choices are:

(1) 'Thesaurus of Classic Jazz' (Philips, mono), a handsome cross-section of New York jazz 1926–30—Nichols, Mole, Bix, the Dorseys, Lang. The first of the four discs is probably the best.

(2) 'Sidney Bechet's Jazz Classics—I' (Blue Note, mono). Some of Bechet's finest sides, including the marvellous 'Blue Horizon,' made in the 'forties with Bunk Johnson, Kaminsky, and Nicholas.

(3) 'Champion Jack Dupree's Natural and Soulful Blues' (London). When Dupree played and sang the blues at Cambridge, the undergraduates tried to start a fund to keep him there. This shows why.

(4) 'Cannonball Takes Charge' (Riverside, mono). It has been Cannonball Adderley's year here, and this disc exhibits his full-throated alto more undilutedly than any.

58
1962 (17 December 1962)

In a year of reissues, 'Condon à la Carte' (Stateside) apotheosises Chicago-style in 1939–40 Commodore tracks new here. 'Sidney Bechet: Giant of Jazz' (Blue Note, two records) enshrines the furiously exciting Bechet-Davison encounters of the 'forties.

Blues lovers should have 'Kings of the Blues' (RCA, three EPs), rare records by classic performers. While 'Charlie Mingus: Jazz Portraits' (United Artists) most represents contemporary jazz with four ebullient and extravagant pieces, one of which is memorably beautiful.

59
1963 (23 December 1963)

All the best records now are reissues (I leave you to guess why), and from the many monumental and scholarly sets I would pick the 3–disc 'King of the Blues Trombone' (Col.), wherein the life of Jack Teagarden unwittingly exemplifies the heyday of white jazz, and the 5–disc 'Charlie Parker Memorial Album' (Realm), a variorum edition of the barrage of experimentalism first mounted by Bird on Dial in the 'forties.

Of current issues, only New Orleans and the Blues have vitality enough to rank with these, and I would pick 'Kid Thomas and his Algiers Stompers' (Riverside) and 'The Legend of Sleepy John Estes' (Esquire) as first-rate examples of their respective kinds.

60
1964 (21 December 1964)

What with that *Time* cover and everything, 1964 was Monk's year, and 'Monk: Big Band And Quartet In Concert' (CBS SBPG 62248) shows off his multi-faceted talent in orchestral, chamber and solo styles. From Yarra, Australia, came 'Fats Waller With The Rhythmmakers' (Swaggie JCS 33764) as if in reply to my appeal last January for a reissue of this whanging Allen-Russell-Condon pick-up group of 1932: jazz shops will help.

With 'Hello, Dolly!' (London SHR 8190) Louis Armstrong beat the Beatles to top place without sacrificing a single nuance of his venerable mastery. For antiquarians, 'Jazz Odyssey Volume One: The Sound of New Orleans' (CBS BPG 62232–4) offers a treasure-chest of Crescent City performers from the ODJB to Bunk Johnson, 48 tracks mostly pre-1930, a cellarful of vintage noise.

61
1965 (20 December 1965)

Veteran Earl Hines scooped the pool this year with a European tour and several fine records, notably 'Spontaneous Explorations' (mono, Stateside SL 10116), to prove his baroque piano as compelling as ever. Nothing could be more different than John Coltrane's 'A Love Supreme' (mono HMV CLP 1869), a four-part attempt by the sheets-of-sound father of the New Thing to say 'Thank You, God' in his own angular fashion, moving from frenzy to faith in doing so. For devotees of the old sophistication, 'The Art Tatum / Ben Webster Quartet' (mono Verve VLP 9090) offers the principals' feathery tenor and meticulously sweeping piano in a miraculously casual bunch of ballads, while for those who are sick of it all 'Scott Joplin 1899–1914' (mono Riverside RM 8815) is a treasure-trove of Edwardian gaiety and pathos by the master of piano-roll ragtime.

62
1966 (19 December 1966)

Since jazz, as I explained some years ago, has now split irrevocably into Negro Art-Music and Beat, it follows that the best records today are either by failing veterans or reissues. Here are four top-class examples of the latter: 'Pee Wee Russell—A Legend' (mono Fontana TL5271), 10 Commodore tracks from the early 'forties, full of raw and practised melodrama; 'Lester Young Leaps Again!' (mono Fontana FJL 128), 1943/44 sessions with Guarnieri and Catlett and the Kansas City Seven which some have called the best Young ever; Count Basie's 'Jumpin' At The Woodside' (mono Ace of Hearts AH111), household words such as 'Every Tub' and 'Doggin' Around' with which the band roared into New York in 1937–38; 'The Bessie Smith Story' (mono CBS BPG62377/80), a monument as massive as the talent it commemorates, 1925–33, with Armstrong, with Henderson, with everybody. But of course you have it already. You *must* have.

63
1967 (18 December 1967)

As reissue programmes grow, today's players have increasingly to struggle against the giants of the 'Thirties and even their own younger selves. 'Things Ain't What They Used To Be' (mono RCA Victor RD 7829) shows Johnny Hodges and the late Rex Stewart with their incomparable 'Ellington Units' of 1940, striking a graceful balance between scoring and solos. 'Billie Holiday: The Golden Years' (mono CBS 66301, 3 discs in box) comprises 48 more tracks from 1935 to 1942 by the young pre-torching Billie whose records were an anthology of all that was elegant in jazz instrumentalists. Ornette Coleman's 'Chappaqua Suite' (mono CBS 66203, 2 discs in pack) is probably the most extended ramble of this philosophic free-former, proving his consistency of conception and inventiveness without recourse to distortion. Finally, 'Jack Teagarden' (mono RCA Victor 7826) is a fascinatingly diverse bunch of tracks—Condon, Waller, Whiteman, Pollack—that might not be everyone's choice. It's mine, though.

64
1968 (16 December 1968)

The jazz record of the year makes it on one side only—the Louis Armstrong half of 'Satchmo Style' (Parlophone PMC 7045), eight numbers with the Luis Russell band of 1929–30, 'St. Louis Blues,' 'Dallas Blues,' 'Bessie Couldn't Help It,' and so on. The Armstrong zenith.

For moderns I pick Monk's 'Work' (Transatlantic Prestige PR 7169), gay and fruitful piano backed up at times by the young, and therefore good, Sonny Rollins. And they might well try 'Miles In The Sky' (CBS 63352), passages of bleak pastoralism delivered with a melancholy and kingly authority.

Don't say you are tired of veteran blues singers without hearing 'Skip James Today' (Vanguard SVRL 19001), whose high voice is swayed by ancient passions like a dead leaf in the wind. My personal naps would be 'Sidney Bechet Sessions' (Storyville 671199), unfamiliar American tracks on which Bechet plays with his peers, and Jimmy Yancey's 'Low Down Dirty Blues' (Atlantic 590018), the last session of this utterly original blues and boogie pianist, helped on occasion by his wife, Estelle 'Mama' Yancey's lyrics. (These are all monos—the Davis is mono/stereo.)

65
1969 (22 December 1969)

The most popular record of the year was Duke Ellington's 'And His Mother Called Him Bill' (RCA SF 7964), the Ducal tribute to the late Billy Strayhorn. Miles Davis's 'Miles In The Sky' (CBS 63352) displayed the cold kingliness of this master, a great contrast to 'Henry "Red" Allen', (RCA RD 8409), wherein the life story of a great trumpeter is told in classics such as 'Feelin' Drowsy.' Waller anthologies abound: 'African Ripples' (RCA RD 8308) is as bountiful a basket as any. My personal nap, however, is 'Condon à la Carte' (Ace of Hearts AH 178). 1938–40 white Chicago-Dixieland stuff, utterly convinced and convincing, the golden end of one particular jazz road.

66
1970 (21 December 1970)

After the single LP, the two-disc, or even three-disc, pack. More reissues than new sessions. The blues avalanche. With the usual caution that I've heard only a fraction of the year's output, I nominate 'Billy Banks and the Rhythmmakers' (CBS/Realm 52732) as the record of the year. Allen, Russell, Waller and the rest in a splendid tumult of 'thirties ad-libbing. Following hard upon it were Art Hodes's 'Sittin' In' (Blue Note B6508) with Kaminsky's classic leads, Ellington's 'Flaming Youth' (RCA RD 8049) and 'Bill Coleman à Paris 1936–38' (Parlophone PMC 7104/5).

For new issues, Ellington's 'Seventieth Birthday Concert' (United Artists UAD 60001) is unbeatable as a keepsake of what must be the final years of this unique organisation, and everyone else seems to like Miles Davis's 'Bitches' Brew' (CBS 66236), so see for yourself. As for the blues, 'J. B. Lenoir' (Polydor Crusade 1) and John Henry Barbee's 'I Ain't Gonna Pick No More Cotton' (Storyville 616013) are both individual and stirring.

Postscript: Larkin's First Essay on Jazz

This 1940 piece was unearthed in the collection of Larkin's papers held at Hull University (PLPBJL). It is referred to and quoted from in Motion's biography (A Writer's Life, 57) but it is not cited in Bloomfield's Bibliography, as it was never published. Nor does Larkin's typescript indicate for whom it was written or where it appeared. We guess that it was another piece for his school magazine, The Coventrian, *to which Larkin contributed a number of pieces from 1933 onwards.*

To offer juvenilia as a Postscript may seem perverse: 'Prescript' would seem a much more appropriate term and locale. We have placed it here for two reasons. The first is that the essay is—to put it with a maximum of charity—not very good: poorly written for the most part, one or two of its sentences are frankly impenetrable, and the tone is solemnly pretentious throughout. It is a commonplace that the style of highly talented adolescents is rarely commensurate with their insight and intellect, and to draw attention to the young Larkin's stylistic frailties is less a gratuitous exposé than proof of how remarkable was his progress thereafter.

Second, there is a raw passion to his proselytising that impresses despite the prose. And not only passion: the claims made for jazz as an indigenous American music are brave and radical. Many years later the great jazz drummer Max Roach would define jazz as 'America's true classical music', and to find Larkin espousing jazz from a similar point of view throws further light on his governing attitudes to the music.

Finally, the date of composition is something of a happy coincidence, in that, three thousand miles away in New York City, the 'new jazz' known as Bebop was burgeoning rapidly. Larkin may have professed a burning dislike for that development on many subsequent occasions, but his words below capture both its significance and (initially difficult) appeal. To celebrate such precocious, albeit unwitting, insight is a fitting way in which to end this collection.

67

The Art of Jazz

Truth can never be told so as to be understood, and not believed.

William Blake

The decay of ritual in everything from religion to the lighting of a fire is resulting in the insulation of the unconscious which finds its daily fulfilment in such ritual. Or, to put it another way, in excising the stages of argument by which conclusions are reached, those conclusions are falsified.

The predicament in which the unconscious is finding itself today is reflected in the general upheaval in all the arts, and particularly in the emergence of a new art, American Jazz music.

Much has been written about Jazz, both enthusiastic and critical. It is denigrated as savage, noisy, mindless, and so on. Even its defenders mistake its stridency for a kind of hieroglyph, and accustom themselves to it as a student learns a foreign language in order to read what has been written by writers in that language.

Nobody sees that the stridency of Jazz is the most important thing about it, for it symbolises the importance and urgency of its problem.

The modern unconscious has chosen to symbolise its predicament of subjugation through the music of a subject people; its predicament of imprisonment through the unvarying monotony of 4/4 rhythm; its panic at its predicament through the arresting texture of the Jazz tone.

The decay of ritual having sundered conscious from unconscious, Jazz is the new art of the unconscious, and is therefore improvised, for it cannot call upon consciousness to express its own divorce from consciousness.

What is the subject-matter of Jazz?

In Jazz the unconscious describes itself almost in its own terms. Though we find it in a certain number of the conventional artistic emotions—the 'moods' of Ellington, the conscious beauty of Beiderbecke, the romanticism of Armstrong—if we move nearer the centre of the music we discover stranger qualities: the pure confidence of Frank Teschmaker [*sic*], the cantabile of Sidney Bechet, and the elemental, dancing gaiety of Pee Wee Russell. Here is the unconscious describing its own beauty and balance, as in Mozart, forever caged in the prison of four beats to the bar.

Can we doubt all this, when we see on all sides this new art gaining an increasing number of enthusiasts among adolescents who would normally be reading poetry or listening to ordinary music? It is not a mere cult of savagery; there is no wide interest evinced by young people of every town in England and the U.S.A. in Negro sculpture or child art. No: the unconscious is in a new state, and has a new need, and has produced a new art to satisfy that need, and it is as well that we should understand.

1940

ADDENDA

68

Melody Maker Jazz Critics' Poll 1965

Philip Larkin's Selections

In February 1965 Larkin was invited to take part in the Melody Maker*'s Critics'*
Poll—something of an honour in those days. Contributors could vote for up to three
musicians in twenty-two categories, and were also invited to cite a 'New Star' and
'Musician of the Year'. Larkin was one of nineteen critics consulted, and the results
were published in the periodical's February 20, 1965 issue.

Some of his choices are as obvious as unexceptionable: Armstrong (twice),
Hodges, Coleman Hawkins, Pee Wee Russell and Ellington. However, the others
compel both attention and comment. While it was obvious from the reviews collected
in All What Jazz *that he respected the musicianship of Freddie Hubbard, Phil*
Woods, Charlie Rouse and Dexter Gordon, Cal Tjader and Roy Haynes, it would be
overstating the case to say that he ever enthused about these post-bop players.

But if those inclusions are surprising, a further six are even more remarkable.
*Given the tone of piece **34**, by turns lukewarm and stern, one would not expect that*
just six years earlier Charles Mingus would be Larkin's Big Band runner-up to
Ellington or his sole citation as bassist. His top pianist is that quintessential bopper,
Bud Powell; Tadd Dameron, no less quintessentially a modernist, is his only
*nominated arranger. And if piece **60** makes his choice of Thelonious Monk as*
Musician of the Year less than extraordinary, the same surely cannot be said for the
appearance of drummer Elvin Jones, the inveterate avant-gardist who for years
fuelled the quartet led by the musician Larkin famously loathed above all others,
John Coltrane.

One must conclude that—as with his 'Record of the Year' choices—Larkin
conscientiously eschewed personal taste, focusing instead on those he felt had made
the most significant contribution to jazz music during the year in question. The
choice of Jones is exemplary: Larkin may have ended up detesting Coltrane's music,

but he took it seriously right up to the tenorist's death in 1967. In All What Jazz *he reviews twenty-one Coltrane records; only Ellington is appraised more often in its pages. Analogously, the seven 'nil returns' do not signify the (absurd) notion that Larkin was not interested in jazz composition or small groups and had no time for the flute or baritone sax; instead, they merely convey the opinion that nothing of any moment had occurred in those categories during the voting-period. One can—many would—disagree about that; that is quite different from inferring that Larkin was interested only in the jazz and the instruments he liked, or indeed that he had no judgment in all other areas.*

Category	*Nominations*
Trumpet	Armstrong, [Freddie] Hubbard, [Clark] Terry
Trombone	Marshall Brown, [Vic] Dickenson, Georg Brunis
Clarinet	Pee Wee Russell, Goodman
Alto Sax	Hodges, Phil Woods, Jimmy Woods
Tenor Sax	Hawkins, Charlie Rouse, Dexter Gordon
Baritone Sax	*None*
Piano	Bud Powell, Junior Mance, Burt Bales
Guitar	Charlie Byrd
Bass	[Charles] Mingus
Drums	Elvin Jones, [Roy] Haynes
Vibes	[Cal] Tjader
Flute	*None*
Organ	Jimmy Smith
Miscellaneous	*None*
Big Band	Ellington, Mingus
Combo	*None*
Arranger	Tadd Dameron
Composer	*None*
Blues/Gospel	Howlin' Wolf, Otis Spann, Lonnie Johnson
Male Singer	Armstrong
Female Singer	*None*
Vocal Group	*None*
Musician of the Year	Thelonious Monk
New Star	Jimmy Woods

69

Lines Written On Louis Armstrong's Death

Part of a 'bundle' housed in the Philip Larkin Room of the Brynmor Jones Library at Hull University, this celebratory threnody has never been published before.

Its provenance has so far proved impossible to establish beyond doubt. The brief Larkin-annotated discography at the end—and the figures which break up the text—suggest it was composed for a radio tribute. A possible reference to it appears in the late B.C. Bloomfield's Philip Larkin: A Bibliography *(Revised Edition; The British Library, 2002): item G22 cites BBC Radio 4's 'The World Tonight' of April 6, 1971. There is only one problem about that: Armstrong did not die until* July 6 *of that year. Bloomfield does add in parentheses, 'Larkin was doubtful whether this was transmitted on the date given in the BBC records,' which seems rather to understate the case. Given the day listed—the 6th—it is possible that the archivist simply transposed the month wrongly.*

That lack of final knowledge is frustrating, but it does not diminish the quality or impact of the piece—especially its final sentence, confirming both Larkin's evaluation of Armstrong as one of the 20th century's greatest artists and the fact that, whatever ludic mischief he got up to in the 'Introduction' to All What Jazz *(and occasionally elsewhere), jazz was his enduring, and perhaps most passionate, love.*

(1)

The news of Louis Armstrong's death will bring sadness to the whole world just as his life brought joy. And I mean the whole world: Tokyo, Johannesburg, Warsaw, Iceland—anywhere you care to mention, this great jazzman, this great entertainer, had his followers and friends. More than anyone, it was Louis Armstrong who, from the operas and spirituals and marches that hummed around his head in New Orleans in the nineteen-hundreds, forged the style of modern popular music, the songs we sing, the rhythms we dance to. In the narrower world of jazz, a whole era, if not the very music itself, comes to an end with him.

I was born the day after Louis received that telegram from King Oliver summoning him to Chicago, and like most of my contemporaries as soon as I was old enough to wind up a gramophone I was sold on his music: West End Blues, Dallas Blues, St.Louis Blues, all of them took hold of my mind like poems, or better than poems, for you were taught those in school, and I had found this wonderful music for myself.

(2)

In many ways Louis, for all his fame, had a hard life. He was born an American Negro in a New Orleans slum. He had no education but what he received in the Coloured Waifs Home. He was an artist, but his art wasn't recognised: he had to create its acceptance, giving two shows a night and then going on by bus or plane, blowing when his lip was shot, never taking a holiday. In the end he became an unofficial, and sometimes official, Ambassador for his country. During the royal progression of his post-war world tours, he had to rely more and more on his voice to carry the show—but what a thrilling, what a human singer he was!

(3)

But don't let's be too sad. Louis wasn't: he lived his life full three-score years and ten, and if he spent them entertaining us, well, 'It's happiness to me,' he once wrote, 'to see people happy. I've a million happy memories.' Remember what he himself said at the death of Fats Waller: 'Fats is gone now . . . but to me he's still here with us. His very good spirit will keep him with us for ages.' That about sums it up for Louis too. He was a great artist of our time, and the music he leaves behind will be our joy for years to come.

(4)

Records

1. Louis Armstrong: His Greatest Years Vol. 4. Parlophone PMC 1150.
'Tight Like This': first chorus and a half of the trumpet solo at the end of the record, following the last piano solo.
2. Same record: 'Muggles': final trumpet solo, two choruses, following clarinet.

3. Louis Armstrong, 'Hello Dolly!' London HA-R 8190
'Moon River': as much of the vocal as you have time for, following the few bars' intro.
4. Louis in Los Angeles, Parlophone PMC 7098
'Sweetheats on Parade'—as much of final trumpet chorus (after the sax break) as time for.

Early July 1971

INDEX

An entry in **bold** type signifies either authorship of a book reviewed or its main subject.

Question what you thought before

Continuum Impacts - books that change the way we think

Continuum
Impacts
CHANGING MINDS

www.continuumbooks.com